THREE COLOURS TRILOGY: BLUE, WHITE, RED

Krzysztof Kieślowski

Krzysztof Piesiewicz

by the same authors

DECALOGUE: THE TEN COMMANDMENTS

of related interest

KIEŚLOWSKI ON KIEŚLOWSKI

THREE COLOURS TRILOGY:
BLUE, WHITE, RED
Krzysztof Kieślowski and
Krzysztof Piesiewicz

Translated by Danusia Stok

faber and faber

First published in 1998
by Faber and Faber Limited
3 Queen Square London WC1N 3AU

Photoset by Parker Typesetting Service, Leicester
Printed in England by Clays Ltd, St Ives plc

A CIP record for this book
is available from the British Library

ISBN 0–571–17892–8

4 6 8 10 9 7 5 3

CONTENTS

NOTE FROM THE TRANSLATOR

Those who are well acquainted with Krzysztof Kieślowski's *Three Colours Trilogy* will notice that, at various points, the films differ from the scripts. This is because, for Kieślowski, filming is a living process, one which should evolve and not stagnate in any preconceived, inflexible framework. Let Kieślowski's words on the relationship between script and film speak for themselves:

> There's an initial sense of why the film is being made, and then, after one, two or five years, the final result appears. And it's only true to the first idea. It's not really identifiable with all that happens later because masses of things happen later. Characters are born, heroes, protagonists, action, the camera comes along, the actors, props, lights and a thousand other things on which you have to compromise. And it's never what you imagine while writing the script, while thinking about the film.
>
> I've got a formula which I worked out a long time ago and which works for me. I always write the whole thing first, whatever it is. I never concentrate on individual scenes, individual solutions individual characters. I write a first version, a sort of intuitive rendering of what the film's going to be about so that the producer knows what the proposal involves. Then I write the treatment, so that the producer can see the scale of the production. This is exceptionally important for me because the treatment contains action or the seeds of action and a sketch of the characters. There's no dialogue yet. Or only scraps of it. Sometimes it's just descriptive. But at any rate, the treatment's another version of the whole. Usually I write two or three versions of a treatment, and only give the third one in. Then I write the script which is about 200 pages long. A page a minute, more or less. I also write two or three versions of the script. I don't write a shooting script. It seems natural that at some time I've got to write dialogue. I think of what the character has to say in the scene and why. And how. I try to imagine the character and think how he'd express himself in just such a situation.

We used to assess each other's scripts in Poland. We'd all show each other films before they were edited or in very rough cuts. To this day, in fact, I discuss every script with Edek Zebrowski or Agnieszka Holland. With *Three Colours* (*Barwy*), which I wrote together with Piesiewicz, we did it more professionally. They agreed to be my script advisors and were paid for it. We'd spend two days on each script, more or less, talking about it. We sat at the first for two days, spent two days on the second, then over two days on the third.

Then the actors come along. Then the cinematographer. And they change a lot of things again. A lot of things are changed before filming. I write another version of the script before the shoot. Then masses of things are changed during the shoot. The actors very often change the dialogue, too; or they tell me that they want to appear in some other scene, because they think that they ought to do or say something else. If they're right, I agree with them.

from *Kieślowski on Kieślowski*,
ed. Danusia Stok, Faber and Faber, 1993

The scripts of the *Three Colours Trilogy* which Krzysztof gave me to translate are the fourth versions.

Danusia Stok, 1998

Three Colours: Blue

CREDITS

EXT. MOTORWAY. DAY (DUSK)

A crowded motorway. Eight lanes of cars speeding in both directions. The rumble of lorries, roar of engines, drone of motorbikes as they weave their way among the cars. Hell.

Against this background: TITLE CREDITS.

The camera tracks downwards and slowly but clearly picks out a speeding navy blue BMW. When the BMW is very near, below the camera – stop frame. Silence. This lasts a second, enough to see – out of focus – a fragment of a man's face at the steering wheel, a woman, also out of focus, laughing at his side, and the outline of a child's face between them in the back. After a second, the image moves, more cars drive past.

EXT. ROAD. DAY (DUSK)

A young man, Antoine, is sitting on his rucksack at the side of a tree-lined, provincial road. His head is tilted as he tries to impale a wooden ball on to the stick which is attached to it with string. A large, professional skateboard is strapped to the rucksack. Antoine has been waiting a long time, he has lost hope of hitching a lift that day. A navy blue BMW approaches from afar at great speed. Antoine, without expectations and without getting up from his rucksack, waves in the direction of the car. The car passes by without slowing down. Antoine nods knowingly. He goes back to his game with the wooden ball which he had interrupted for a moment. A few attempts and, with a dry crack, the ball jumps into place. At that moment we hear a loud crash. Antoine looks away from his ball. He turns around. A few hundred metres in front of him, at the road's bend, a navy blue BMW is wrapped around a roadside tree. Dust starts to descend from the side of the road. The BMW sways for a few moments, then comes to a standstill, surrounded by steam from the shattered radiator. A branch falls from the tree, torn by the crash. Antoine, skateboard under his arm, runs quickly in the direction of the accident. From a distance, we see him approach the car and try to open the door.

3

INT. HOSPITAL. MONITORING STATION. DAY

A room with a number of hospital monitors. An Older Doctor, a Younger Doctor and a Nurse are leaning over one of them. The body they are watching is functioning normally. They look at the monitor intently for a moment.

OLDER DOCTOR
I'm going in to see her.

He leaves the room. The Younger Doctor and the Nurse stay by the monitor.

INT. HOSPITAL. DAY

The Older Doctor leans over Julie. He looks at her intently, anxiously. Julie's shoulder is immobilized by an armour-like plaster-cast and her eyelid is lacerated.

OLDER DOCTOR
How are you?

Julie nods, not bad. She looks all right, despite the pipes and intravenous drip attached to her. The Doctor doesn't leave his place by her head. He takes a deep breath.

During the . . . were you conscious?

Julie nods again, yes, she was conscious.

I have to . . . You know?

Julie confirms with a weak nod. The Doctor, however, wants to be certain that Julie does indeed know what she should.

Your husband died in the accident.

Julie indicates, lowering her eyelids, that she knows. Then she suddenly opens her eyes and fixes them sharply, anxiously, at the Doctor's face. The Doctor bites his lips.

You must have been unconscious some . . .

JULIE
I don't know . . . Anna?

4

INT. HOSPITAL. MONITORING STATION. DAY

The line showing the patient's heartbeat on the monitor rapidly changes. The Younger Doctor and the Nurse watch the quivering line anxiously.

INT. HOSPITAL. DAY

> OLDER DOCTOR

Yes. Your daughter too.

Julie closes her eyes tightly. The Doctor observes her for a while, then leaves. The sound of a door closing; Julie keeps her eyes closed.

INT. HOSPITAL. DAY

The Older Doctor enters the room. He approaches the Younger Doctor and the Nurse who are leaning over the monitor. The quivering lines on the screen slowly calm down and then, alarmingly, take off again.

> OLDER DOCTOR

It's normal.

The Younger Doctor nods.

We'll take her off in the morning.

INT. HOSPITAL. NIGHT

Julie gets up from the bed and, still somewhat clumsy in her movements, removes the flowers (a beautiful blue bouquet) from a vase on the table. She judges the weight of the vase in her hands – it is heavy enough. She leaves the room carrying the vase. Night, the corridors are empty. Julie sees the light on in the nurses' room and, beyond the light, a bend in the corridor. She walks past the nurses' room, stooping a little. She sees the Nurse leaning over a tray used for preparing medication. She follows the bend in the corridor, passes the toilet. Around the corner there is another corridor leading to a window. Julie approaches the window, stops at the appropriate distance, and with difficulty – because of the plaster-cast – takes a swing, throwing the vase at the glass. A crash, the shattering of broken glass. Julie backs away to the toilet. Through the half-open door, she sees the Nurse run past. She leaves the toilet and enters the nurses' room. She looks around, finds the medicine cabinet. It is locked. Julie looks around, sees a small key beside the medication tray. The key fits the cabinet. Julie opens the cabinet, finds a bottle of Rohipnolem. She empties out a handful of pills. She is in a hurry now. She locks the cabinet and puts the key in its place. She hears the nurse running towards her. She stands beside the door. The Nurse bursts into the room. Excited, she does not notice Julie. She grabs the telephone and dials. She speaks a little too loudly.

NURSE

Mr Leroy, call the police. Somebody's smashed the window in corridor B on the first floor. And come right away . . .

Julie, taking advantage of the Nurse's distraction, slips through the half-open door. She returns to her room, gets back into bed. For some time, she listens to the sound of footsteps and the noise in the corridor. Then she opens her slightly sweaty palm. Slowly, she brings it up to her lips. When it looks as if she is going to swallow all the pills, she suddenly closes her palm. She reaches for the bell. The Nurse arrives. Still agitated, she stands in the door.

JULIE

Come closer, please.

The Nurse approaches. Julie shows her her open palm full of pills.

I took them . . . But I can't. I'm unable to . . .

The Nurse gently takes the pills, one by one, from Julie's hand. Julie does not look at her. After a while she opens her eyes.

I broke the window in the corridor.

NURSE

Don't worry. They'll replace it.

JULIE

I'm sorry.

The Nurse goes up to the door, opens it. She turns to Julie.

NURSE

I'll keep the door open.

Julie nods, but when the Nurse leaves she gets up and quietly closes the door. Then she goes back to bed and buries her head in the pillow. By the trembling of her shoulders we can see that she is crying. The telephone on the table rings. Julie does not react. The telephone rings a few times, then finally falls silent. Julie sobs desperately.

INT. TELEVISION SHOP. DAY

A Saleslady in the television shop is unpacking a miniature television set from a box. She plugs the TV in and shows it to Olivier. Olivier is thirty-five and has a quiet face. The Saleslady plays with the aerial to get a good picture.

SALESLADY
You change channels here. Brightness, colour, volume . . .

The Saleslady shows Olivier the respective knobs. Olivier listens attentively for a moment, then suddenly turns his eyes away. He blinks, as if buying the television is causing him pain.

INT. HOSPITAL. DAY

Julie is asleep. She wakes with the feeling of somebody watching her. Olivier is sitting by the bed. He leans towards her hand and touches her palm. Julie looks at his lowered head; does not withdraw her hand. Olivier gets up and for a moment longer holds Julie's palm in his hands. Then he reaches into his pocket, takes out the tiny television set and hands it to Julie. Julie does not know much about technical things and does not know what it is for. Olivier presses a button and, for a moment, on the small screen we see a contest of brightly coloured climbers on a rock face. Realizing the obvious inappropriateness of the image, Olivier turns the television off. Julie looks at him questioningly.

JULIE
Is it today?

Olivier nods.

OLIVIER
This evening . . .

Julie holds on to the television. Olivier, sensing that his visit is over, gets up and moves towards the door.

Is there anything I can do?

JULIE

Take the phone.

Olivier goes back, takes the telephone from the table, unplugs it, carefully winds the cable around it. He thinks it over for a moment then replaces the telephone and plugs it back in.

OLIVIER

You might need it.

INT. HOSPITAL. NIGHT

Julie's hand reaches out for the tiny television lying on the table. Moving the arm which is poking out of the plaster armour with difficulty, she pulls the quilt over her head. In this way, she has built herself a kind of tent. Under it, she turns on the television. She moves it around a little and the picture becomes clear. We see a report from the funeral. Two coffins, a large one and a small one, stand on the catafalque. A cushion with orders and awards lies beside the large one. A sextet of young musicians is playing a touching melody.

COMMENTATOR
(*TV voice-over*)

This is a march by the deceased's favourite composer, Van den Budenmayer. It is being played by students from the Academy of Music who bid their professor farewell.

The Minister of Culture steps forward. The music fades to silence.

MINISTER
(*on TV*)

Ladies and gentlemen. Today we bid farewell to a man and composer whom all the press, on writing about his death, described as 'the greatest'. World music will not recover quickly from this unnecessary and unexpected death. We, who were honoured with his friendship, can but bow our heads over the injustice of this death. Patrick . . . The entire world, and especially we here in Europe, awaited your music . . .

Julie is not listening to the speech. She is looking at the coffins and, with her finger, touches first the larger, then the smaller one on the screen.

8

She frames the screen with her fingers so that she sees only the smaller coffin. When the Minister of Culture pronounces her husband's name, she turns the television so that the picture wavers and blurs and then quivering black and white dots cover the screen. Julie looks at the screen now with a clear decision in her eyes.

INT. HOSPITAL. DAY

There are no traces of the accident on Julie's face anymore. A bandage has taken the place of the plaster armour around her shoulder. Julie is sitting in the doctor's consulting room. She reaches for the packet of cigarettes on the table.

JULIE

May I?

DOCTOR

Are you asking me as a doctor? Or as the owner of the packet?

Julie does not smile at the joke, although she should. She pulls out a cigarette.

You shouldn't . . .

Julie nods. She lights up without particular pleasure, inhales and, after a moment, stubs it out in the ashtray. The Doctor is looking through his notes.

Today *La Sept* and *L'Évènement du Jeudi* called. That makes it the thirteenth and fourteenth request for an interview . . .

Julie shakes her head.

I'm not asking, just telling you. I said you'd probably say no.

JULIE

Quite right.

DOCTOR

I'd like you to make one exception. She's an intelligent woman. I know she's not looking for anything sensational. You should meet her.

JULIE

No.

DOCTOR

It would be a good idea from a medical point of view. You can't lose touch with people completely . . .

Julie answers quickly and decidedly, without raising her voice.

JULIE

I said no.

INT./EXT. HOSPITAL. DAY

Julie is lying on the terrace in a comfortable deckchair. The door to her room is open. The terrace is quite large, partitioned by high balustrades made of blue glass. Julie is looking somewhere in front of her, she has put the book (published by Laffont) she is reading aside. A ray of sunshine pierces the blue glass and falls on her face. She closes her eyes. At that moment, loud music resounds. It seems to last only seconds. When she opens her eyes, sensing somebody's eyes on her, the music stops. Leaning over the balustrade from the neighbouring part of the terrace, and tilting her head, an older, well-dressed woman is looking at her. When the woman speaks in a friendly tone, Julie recognizes her. The woman is a Journalist.

JOURNALIST

Hello . . .

JULIE

Hello.

JOURNALIST

I know you don't want to see me . . .

JULIE

No.

The Journalist is obviously prepared for such a turn in the conversation.

JOURNALIST

That publisher . . .

Julie looks at the book she has been reading and which the Journalist is indicating.

JULIE

Laffont . . .

JOURNALIST

Laffont. They are proposing you write a book – *My Life with Patrick*. You won't, I know. Even if they paid you a million.

JULIE

No, I won't.

JOURNALIST

They asked me to ask you.

JULIE

So now you've asked.

Julie gets up from the deckchair, closes her book. The Journalist stops her.

JOURNALIST

Julie, it's not for an interview.

JULIE

What then?

JOURNALIST

I'm writing an article about your husband for *Le Monde de la Musique*. I won't write that I've talked to you. There's one thing I don't know . . .

JULIE

What?

JOURNALIST

What state is the Concert for the Unification of Europe in?

Julie looks at the Journalist for a moment.

JULIE

It doesn't exist.

JOURNALIST

You've changed. You were never so abrasive or unpleasant.

JULIE

Maybe . . .

JOURNALIST

What's happened?

JULIE

Don't you know? We had a car crash. My daughter was killed. So was my husband.

Julie turns away, moves towards the door of her room, her book and blanket under her arm. The Journalist lifts a small camera to her eye and snaps. Julie disappears into her room and closes the door.

INT. DEAN'S ROOM AT THE ACADEMY OF MUSIC. DAY

Olivier clears the desk in the dean's office at the Academy of Music. He puts all the papers, letters and documents found in the desk drawers into a folder. For a moment he hesitates whether to put a series of photographs he has found at the back of the drawer into the folder too. A forty-year-old man (Patrick) with a young woman (Sandrine) appears on them. Olivier makes a decision, puts the photographs in with the rest of the papers and fastens the now crammed folder.

INT./EXT. HOSPITAL. DAY

Julie says goodbye to the Doctor in his consulting room. Olivier, with his crammed folder, and the Lawyer, who have obviously come to collect her, are also present. Julie is dressed in her own clothes; she has evidently been discharged. She shakes hands with the Doctor.

DOCTOR

I think that check-ups are absolutely necessary over the next six months. Every month, then less frequently. You ought to take up some sort of sport.

JULIE

I'll call.

In turn, Olivier and the Lawyer say goodbye to the Doctor. In the meantime, Julie glances outside, no doubt wanting to see what the weather is like. She notices several television reporters with cameras, a few photographers, some with microphones and several journalists with tape-recorders in front of the main entrance to the hospital. She turns to the Doctor.

Call the police, please.

The Doctor shrugs helplessly.

DOCTOR

I did ask them . . . But they've got a right to stand there.

Julie thinks it over for a moment.

JULIE

Excuse me.

She goes out of the consulting rooms leaving the three men there. A moment later Olivier catches up with her in the corridor.

OLIVIER

Wait here. I'll get rid of them.

JULIE

I'll manage.

She moves away, but Olivier calls after her.

OLIVIER

I'll get rid of them!

Julie turns into a side corridor and reaches some stairs marked 'Emergency Exit'. With her light bag slung over her shoulder, she runs down the stairs.

EXT. IN FRONT OF THE HOSPITAL. DAY

Julie exits by the hospital side entrance. A taxi is standing in front of it with its motor running. Beside the taxi, the same female Journalist smiles at a surprised Julie.

JOURNALIST

I called you a taxi.

JULIE

Thanks.

She gets inside the car, leans out of the window.

Do you want a lift?

JOURNALIST

I've got my car. Thanks.

Julie gives the driver an address and the taxi moves away from the hospital.

EXT. JULIE'S HOUSE. DAY

The taxi stops in front of the drive of a house surrounded by a garden. Julie pays and gets out. She crosses the garden. The Gardener turns off his hedge-trimmer. Surprised by her sudden appearance, he nods in greeting and does not quite know what to do. He stands helpless, with the now redundant machine in his hands. Julie walks up to him.

JULIE

Good morning. What're you doing?

GARDENER

Good morning. I wanted everything to be . . .

JULIE

No need.

> GARDENER

We're all deeply sorry . . .

> JULIE

I know. Thank you.

She leans over towards the Gardener and asks.

Have you cleared out Anna's room? Like I asked?

The Gardener lowers his head.

> GARDENER

Yes.

> JULIE

You've got rid of everything?

> GARDENER

Everything.

Julie moves towards the house. The Maid opens the door for her.

INT. JULIE'S HOUSE. DAY

*The Maid is a big woman with a calm, severe face. She is about fifty.
She opens the door and greets Julie without a smile. She shows her a
piece of paper covered in writing lying on the table.*

> MAID

I noted all the phone calls . . .

Julie shrugs.

There's a whole tape of messages on the answering machine.

*Julie goes up to the telephone, removes the tape from the answering
machine, picks up the annotated slip of paper lying next to the
telephone, tears it up and throws everything into the rubbish bin in the
kitchen. The Maid follows closely behind her. She does not react to
anything that Julie does and stops at the bottom of the stairs when Julie
goes upstairs. Feeling her eyes on her, Julie runs lightly up the stairs. At
the top, she slows down. She approaches the open door of the nursery.
For a moment she looks at the empty room, painted blue, and at the
round lamp of the same colour hanging from the ceiling, and*

immediately pushes the door shut. She enters the bedroom, which is in perfect order. She goes through the bathroom into a large study. There is a huge grand piano there, an ordinary piano and a number of electronic instruments. Julie looks around for a moment, searches for something on a shelf stacked with files of musical scores, does not find it. On the piano she notices a piece of paper with one line of notes written on it. She reads them briefly, folds the paper in four and hides it in her small bag. A sound stops her. She listens carefully. It is an almost silent weeping, coming from a distance. Julie leaves the study and, looking for the source of the weeping, quietly goes down the stairs. The weeping gets louder, yet there is nobody in the kitchen. She sees the door of the small larder slightly ajar. Trying not to make any noise, she approaches and opens the door a little wider. With her back to her, so large in the tiny larder, stands the Maid. Leaning her head on a shelf full of jars, she cries wretchedly. Julie watches her for a moment without any expression.

JULIE

Why are you crying, Marie?

MAID

Because you're not.

Julie hesitates for a moment, taken aback by the simplicity of the answer, then holds out her arms. The Maid immediately puts her arms around her and now they both stand in the cramped larder. The Maid, nestling close, cries like a child. Julie's eyes are dry and she looks somewhere into the distance. She delicately strokes the Maid's wide shoulders, slowly calms her down.

I remember them, God, I remember everything . . . When will I ever forget?

The Maid's sobbing, growing quieter, can still be heard as Julie heavily returns upstairs. She sits down on the top stair with her legs wide apart. Through the corner of her eye she notices that the door to Anna's room is still ajar. She stretches out her arm and slams it shut with all her might. The crying downstairs grows silent. Julie now sits with her head in her hands. She hears an approaching car, a door slamming, the bell. She hears the Maid's shuffle, the front door opening. Julie does not move, does not change her position.

16

Olivier and the Lawyer enter the drawing-room.

MAID
(*from the door*)
Would you like something to drink?

Both men thank her, they don't want anything. The Lawyer places his large briefcase on the table, Olivier has the crammed folder in his hand. They sit down on the edge of their armchairs, without making themselves comfortable. They both become aware of this at the same time. The Lawyer smiles faintly.

LAWYER
Shall we sit comfortably? This could take a while.

He sits deeper into the armchair. Olivier stays as he was. For some time they sit in silence. Olivier gets up with the folder in his hand.

OLIVIER
Excuse me.

Julie is still sitting motionless on the stairs with her head in her hands. After a while we hear light footsteps approaching. From the bend in the stairs Olivier emerges, the folder in his hand. Surprised by her presence, he stops. They look at each other. Feeling that he has seen something he should not have, something indiscreet, Olivier backs away without taking his eyes off her. Julie continues to sit for a moment, sighs, gets up and goes downstairs. Olivier and the Lawyer get up from their armchairs in the drawing-room. Olivier shows her the folder he is holding.

I took this from Patrick's office at the Academy. His papers, letters, photographs . . . I wanted to leave it upstairs . . .

JULIE
I don't need it.

Olivier puts the folder on the sideboard.

Take it, please.

Olivier picks up the folder again. He opens it and goes through the papers and photographs. After some thought, he closes the folder.

OLIVIER

I thought it would interest you. I'm here if you need me.

Olivier smiles, shakes hands with the Lawyer and leaves, bowing to Julie. Julie pours two glasses of wine and hands one to the Lawyer. The Lawyer opens his leather briefcase, takes out a wad of documents.

LAWYER

There's a whole lot of things. I don't know if you're fit to . . .

JULIE

I am.

LAWYER

During . . . your illness, life went on as usual. We finalized the purchase of your flat in New York. Our stockbroker rightly invested quite a fair amount of money in Hungarian government debts . . .

Julie stops him.

JULIE

Good. I'll make things easier for you . . . How many digits are there in our bank account number?

LAWYER

Nine . . .

JULIE

Let's think of a number with nine digits . . .

LAWYER

I don't understand. I don't know how . . .

JULIE

It's very simple. When's your birthday?

LAWYER

Twenty-seven, six, forty-one

JULIE

That's six digits. How old is your daughter?

LAWYER

Nineteen.

JULIE

That's eight. Now . . . let's say; how many teeth have you got missing?

The Lawyer, worried and surprised, counts with his tongue.

LAWYER

Five.

JULIE

That gives us nine digits. The number of this secret account is 270641195.

The Lawyer cannot understand Julie's intentions. Still, because he is scrupulous, he does not stop running his tongue over his teeth.

LAWYER

Sorry, six. I've got six teeth missing.

JULIE

Right. So the number is: 270641196. Note that down. Pay all the money from all our banks into this account. I ask you for absolute discretion. No one must ever know. That's very important to me.

The Lawyer is panting. He is desperately looking for some sort of argument.

LAWYER

I've got to know the owner's name. To pay money into an account . . .

JULIE

You'll find out.

LAWYER

Yes. I'll find out.

JULIE

First, you'll pay for my mother's rest-home for the rest of her life.

LAWYER

Yes.

JULIE

You'll return all the advances resulting from contracts reasonably soon. We're not going to be able to honour them.

LAWYER

We can keep them, according to the contracts.

JULIE

You'll return them. Next you'll sell all our shares and also the Hungarian government debts. You'll sell the house, all our possessions and cars, the flat in New York and the house on the coast. All the money will go to the same account.

LAWYER

270641196?

JULIE

Yes.

LAWYER

To someone we don't know?

JULIE

Yes.

LAWYER

That's millions.

JULIE

Yes.

LAWYER

May I ask you why?

JULIE

No.

The Lawyer, annoyed, gets up from the armchair.

LAWYER

Would you excuse me a moment?

He leaves the room and quite obviously disappears into the toilet. Julie smiles faintly. She gets up, again pours wine into both glasses. We hear the toilet flush. The lawyer returns, smiling unpleasantly.

20

What will you have left?

JULIE

My own account.

The Lawyer nods with the same unpleasant smile on his face. He raises his glass, drinks a little wine, grimaces as if he does not like it much. For the first time he thinks he has an idea concerning Julie's instructions.

LAWYER

We'll have to wait for the settlement of the will. I can't do any of this before.

Julie speaks as calmly as before.

JULIE

Right, we'll wait.

INT./EXT. JULIE'S HOUSE. DUSK

In the blue light of the ending day, Julie sighs and opens her handbag. She takes out the folded score sheet, spreads it out. She looks carefully at the individual notes. Her eyes return to the first note and she begins anew. Clear, loud strokes on a piano are heard, each corresponding to the note which Julie is looking at. It is a fragment from a concerto (about twenty seconds). She takes her eyes off the sheet of paper but the music continues, perhaps the orchestration becomes even more complicated. Julie looks to the side. She sees her finger next to the rod supporting the grand piano lid. Slowly, she moves her finger towards the rod, then equally slowly pushes the rod which finally slips along the smooth surface of the grand piano and the lid crashes down. At that moment the music stops. Julie is breathing a little faster. She folds the sheet in four and puts it in her handbag. She turns on the lamp, goes up to the window, leans against the casement and looks in front of her. Through the window she sees the garden, old trees in the falling dusk, the alley and, somewhere in the distance, Paris.

The camera tracks in, losing Julie. We now see only what is beyond the window. The park slowly grows darker in front of our eyes. In a matter of a few seconds, it is night. At the same time as the park darkens, Julie's face, lit by the lamp, appears in the reflection. With the image of her face, the same music as before breaks out. Julie closes her eyes.

EXT. STREET OUTSIDE THE COPYIST'S FLAT. DAY

Julie stops her small sports car, backs in and parks on the pavement near some café tables on the street. She gets out and enters the front door of the building. We can see that she knows the place.

INT. STAIRWELL. DAY

Julie waits for the lift. She realizes that somebody is using the lift because the red light is flickering steadily. Obviously losing patience, she runs up the stairs. Near the second floor, the illuminated lift, majestically descending, passes her. Julie rings at a door on the fourth floor. The door is opened by a young woman, the Copyist.

INT. THE COPYIST'S FLAT. DAY

The room is cluttered with music scores, scrolls of music paper and old etchings, which the Copyist obviously loves – they hang everywhere.

> COPYIST
> I hadn't started yet . . . I spread the work out the day . . .

Julie makes it easier for her.

> JULIE
> The day I left?

> COPYIST
> Yes. Then I thought I'd wait to hear from you.

> JULIE
> You were right.

The Copyist takes out several score sheets in large format. She spreads them out. The score is marked with a large number of corrections made with a blue felt-tip pen. The Copyist points to the blue marks.

> COPYIST
> A lot of corrections . . .

> JULIE
> Same as usual, more or less.

The Copyist hands the score to Julie. It is obvious that she is sorry to part with it.

COPYIST

It's beautiful.

Julie smiles faintly. She nods, maybe it is. She rolls up the score.

JULIE

Any news? Have you heard from him?

COPYIST

No. In fact . . . I've got used to being alone.

Julie gets ready to leave with the score roll under her arm.

JULIE

He'll come back. They usually do.

Something suddenly occurs to the Copyist. She stops Julie.

COPYIST

You didn't bump into each other?

JULIE

Who?

COPYIST

She was here . . . she left just before you came. Ms Gaudry from *Le Monde de la Musique*. I thought you might have bumped into each other in the lift.

JULIE

No . . .

She goes up to the window and looks out at the street but nothing attracts her attention. She sees her car and the coloured parasols of the café. The usual traffic. She does not see the Journalist.

COPYIST

She wanted to talk about my work, but while we were talking I realized that she was after something else.

JULIE

This?

She indicates the score roll. The Copyist nods, yes that.

Did you tell her?

23

The Copyist shakes her head.

> COPYIST
> They're delicate matters.

> JULIE
> Thanks. I don't know whether we'll see each other again . . .

She holds out her hand to the Copyist. The Copyist shakes it, smiles.

> COPYIST
> Don't bank on it.

INT. STAIRWELL. DAY

Julie runs down the stairs with the score. On the landing, the view from the window on to the yard stops her. Dustbin men are dragging rubbish bins to the droning rubbish truck in the middle of the yard.

EXT. YARD. DAY

Julie, with the score in her hand, runs up to a dustbin man who is dragging a plastic bin. Just before he puts it into the clasps of the rubbish truck, she throws the roll into the bin. The dustbin man smiles at her haste and pulls the handle. Julie stands for a while and watches as the truck grinds the contents of the bin with an unpleasant crunch.

EXT. STREET OUTSIDE THE COPYIST'S FLAT. DAY

Julie walks up to her car and notices the Journalist, Ms Gaudry, sitting in the café. The Journalist smiles at Julie as if she has been waiting for her. Julie hesitates, opens then closes her car door. She approaches the smiling Journalist, greets her, but does not sit down.

> JOURNALIST
> Funny coincidence, isn't it?

> JULIE
> It is.

She looks around. She is sure that the Journalist could not have seen her throwing the score into the rubbish truck.

JOURNALIST

I thought you'd come here. Then when I left and saw your car, I thought my intuition's pretty good.

Julie nods at her intelligence or shrewdness.

JULIE

It's not the interview or the book?

JOURNALIST

No.

JULIE

What then?

JOURNALIST

Give me half an hour and I'll explain.

JULIE

I won't.

She makes a move to leave immediately. The Journalist's voice stops her.

JOURNALIST

A scar.

JULIE

I'm sorry?

JOURNALIST

There was a scar on the inside of his thigh.

She pulls the chair back, sits down.

JULIE

How do you know?

JOURNALIST

Will you give me a moment?

JULIE

How do you know?!

JOURNALIST

Don't worry. We used to play in the sandpit together. Then I read about him, then I wrote. There's no more to it than that.

JULIE

What do you want to know?

JOURNALIST

How the talented young man became outstanding.

JULIE

That's a lot.

JOURNALIST

I know you organized his life. You paid his taxes, drew up his contracts. He didn't have to think about deadlines, tickets or meetings. That was reflected in his will. You've inherited everything.

JULIE

You know a lot.

JOURNALIST

Yes. I've spoken to a lot of people. Including Olivier.

JULIE

Olivier?

JOURNALIST

Olivier. I noticed he enjoyed talking about you. He worked with your husband long enough, so he knows. He said you had a good marriage. That you're calm, warm . . .

Julie does not say anything, looks away. The Journalist leans towards her.

Did you love each other?

JULIE

Yes, very much.

JOURNALIST

And that was enough? Love?

JULIE

I guess . . .

The Journalist looks at Julie closely, intently.

JOURNALIST

What I really want to know is, did you write Patrick's music?

Julie doesn't hesitate for a moment.

JULIE

No.

INT. JULIE'S HOUSE. DUSK

There is no longer any furniture in the house. In the light of a lamp standing on the floor, Julie empties her handbag of everything one usually finds in a woman's bag. Carefully she sorts it out, making two piles, one with the things she has decided to keep (her passport, the folded music score, a manicure set) and a separate pile with what she has decided to throw away (various keys, an address book, small notes, the tiny television set she got from Olivier). She brings a waste-paper basket over and puts everything she wants to throw away into it. She shakes the handbag out upside down. Some dust floats out and a coloured lollipop. Julie stops motionless. She bends over and picks up the lollipop. A rustle of cellophane. She closes her eyes, then, after a while, opens them. She takes off the cellophane and tastes. She licks the surface of the lolly several times then suddenly, with a crunch, bites it to pieces and swallows it. She puts the handbag aside and reaches for the telephone. She takes the address book from the waste-paper basket, finds a number. She punches out the number and, waiting for the tone, throws the address book back into the basket. A man's voice answers on the other end of the line.

OLIVIER
(*off*)

Hello . . .

JULIE

It's Julie. I wanted to ask you . . . Do you love me?

A moment's silence.

OLIVIER
(*off*)

Yes.

                              JULIE
Since when?

INTERCUT WITH OLIVIER'S FLAT. DUSK

Olivier in his flat with the telephone receiver at his ear. In the background we can see a grand piano. It is a large, decent flat.

                              OLIVIER
Since I started working with Patrick.

He wipes his sweaty palm on his shirt then reaches for a cigarette.

INT. JULIE'S HOUSE. DUSK

                              JULIE
                        (*on the telephone*)
Do you think I'm wonderful?

                              OLIVIER
                            (*off*)
Yes.

                              JULIE
Fascinating?

                              OLIVIER
                            (*off*)
Yes.

                              JULIE
Do you think of me? Will you miss me?

                              OLIVIER
                            (*off*)
Yes . . .

                              JULIE
Then come.

                              OLIVIER
                            (*off*)
Now?

JULIE

Yes, now.

For a moment Olivier remains silent on the phone.

OLIVIER
(*off; emotionless*)

Are you sure?

Now it's Julie who does not reply immediately.

JULIE

Come.

INTERCUT WITH OLIVIER'S FLAT. DUSK

Olivier puts down the receiver. We see the mist of sweat from his palm slowly disappear from the black plastic.

INT. JULIE'S HOUSE. NIGHT

It must be pouring outside because Olivier stands in the door completely drenched. His hair is plastered down with rain, his coat heavy with water and the right side of his trousers muddy. Julie looks at him, tilting her head. She is wearing a short, dark, stretch dress and is barefoot.

OLIVIER

I slipped and fell . . .

JULIE

Take it off.

Olivier, without taking his eyes off Julie, unbuttons and takes off his coat, looks around for somewhere to hang it, but there is no furniture in the house any more. Encouraged by Julie's gesture, he simply drops the coat on the floor. The tension between them, present from the beginning of the scene, increases.

And the rest . . .

Olivier unbuttons his shirt and pulls it out of his trousers. He does not feel comfortable undressing under Julie's eyes. In order to undo his trouser belt, he has to look down. At that moment, Julie pulls her dark,

stretch dress over her head with one move and takes it off. Olivier, his hand on his trouser belt, lifts his eyes, stops short. Julie lets him look.

They've already taken the bed. Only the mattress is left.

She goes up to Olivier and cuddles up in such a way that Olivier naturally picks her up in his arms. Julie has her arms around his neck. Olivier moves in the direction of the mattress and slowly lays Julie down.

INT. JULIE'S HOUSE. NIGHT

Julie watches Olivier's sleeping face. After a while she speaks in a whisper.

> JULIE
> Olivier, are you asleep? Olivier . . .

Olivier does not answer or move. Julie shifts her eyes, and looks ahead somewhere into the distance. She continues speaking in a whisper.

It could even be like this. But it won't.

Olivier does not move. Julie, her head resting on her arm, closes her eyes. She takes a deep breath and for a moment holds the air in her lungs, does not let it go, just as one does when one wants to swim under water as far as possible.

INT. JULIE'S HOUSE. DAWN

Julie, dressed in jeans and a shirt, places a cup of coffee by the mattress. Olivier, smelling the hot coffee, opens his eyes. Still not completely conscious, he sees Julie in front of him ready to go out.

> JULIE
> I appreciate what you did for me. I take it you won't miss me. You must have noticed there's nothing to miss. I'm just like any other woman. I sweat. I cough at night. I had a toothache in the early hours. I've got a cavity.

She smiles faintly, picks up a large, leather bag and leaves the room. She throws it at him from the door.

Shut the door when you leave.

She disappears through the door so quickly that Olivier does not manage to do or say anything. Only after a while does he realize what has happened. He looks for his trousers, finds them quite a way from the mattress, pulls them on and runs up to the window. He opens it. He sees Julie's sports car in front of the house and Julie herself disappearing through the open gate. She cannot hear him shout any more.

OLIVIER

Julie!

EXT. IN FRONT OF JULIE'S HOUSE. DAY

Julie walks briskly alongside the wall of her house. She brings her clenched fist against the wall and drags the knuckles along it. This lasts for a while. She stops. She pulls her fist away from the wall. Torn skin, blood collecting. She hisses with pain, tears in her eyes. Instinctively, she brings the injured knuckles to her lips. She continues towards the busy crossroads visible ahead.

INT. METRO STATION. DAY

Julie gets off at the last metro station. She is wearing jeans and has a small rucksack on her back. All the passengers get off, it is obviously the last station. Julie makes her way in the crowd towards the exit.

EXT. PARIS SUBURBS. DAY

Together with the crowd, Julie emerges from the station. She looks around, pleased. The buildings here are not as tall as in the centre of Paris; a market square full of little shops, fruit and fish stalls, a lot of people, many of whom know each other. A buzz. For a moment Julie disappears from our eyes, then we find her again, looking at the houses, shops, people. She stops in front of a small display of notices about apartments for sale. She looks at them, goes in.

INT. ESTATE AGENTS. DAY

The Proprietor is well dressed, thirty-something. He takes advantage of his good looks with a certain dignity. He now listens carefully to Julie.

JULIE

Not large, three rooms, can be on the top floor. Can be without a lift.

The Proprietor considers this.

PROPRIETOR

A bit of exercise?

JULIE

You could put it that way. I'd like a terrace. Or a big balcony . . .

PROPRIETOR

I've got what you're looking for . . . Excuse me, but it would be easier for me to advise you. What do you do?

JULIE

Nothing.

PROPRIETOR

Nothing at all?

JULIE

Nothing at all.

The Proprietor gently rubs the tip of his nose. The gesture suits him. Julie smiles innocently. The Proprietor takes out a pen.

PROPRIETOR

Your name, please.

JULIE

Julie de Coursy.

The Proprietor starts to note this down.

JULIE

Sorry, that was automatic. I'm going back to my maiden name. Julie Vignon.

INT./EXT. JULIE'S FLAT. DUSK

Julie looks over the district from the terrace of her new flat. We see rooftops and neighbours' apartments. Julie stretches; she is in a good mood. *In the window opposite, someone with their back to her is sitting in an armchair watching TV. On TV we see a mountaineering competition. The contestants, colourfully dressed, make use of every crevice in the artificial rock. Julie turns away from the TV. She goes back inside through the open balcony door. The flat is still completely empty, redecorated, the walls clean. In the furnished kitchen, Julie finds a stool. She places it in the middle of the room, climbs up on to it. She stretches up to see if she can reach the hook in the middle of the ceiling. The stool is high enough. From the bag standing on the windowsill, Julie pulls out the blue globe of the lamp which we already know. She climbs on to the stool again and hangs the lamp. From the bag she also pulls out a black jumper and a skirt on hangers. She hangs them on the door. She approaches the window, puts the empty bag back on the sill. Within the cityscape she sees the dome of a swimming pool. She smiles, nods.*

INT. SWIMMING POOL. NIGHT

The pool is empty at this hour. The blue light reflects against the surface of the water. Julie dives in. With calm strokes, she conquers the entire length of the pool.

EXT. PARIS SUBURBS. DAY

Julie is sitting under a café parasol. The streets and market place are crowded. A Waiter walks past.

> WAITER
> *(in passing)*

Okay?

> JULIE

Okay. And you?

The Waiter nods, he is okay too. On his way back, he slows down a little alongside Julie.

> WAITER

Same as usual?

> JULIE

Same.

The Waiter goes and, as she waits, Julie leans over to see what she usually evidently observes from this spot. A man wearing a coat stops beside a wall, pulls out a flute and begins to play, thinly. The Waiter brings ice-cream and coffee. Julie pours a little of the coffee into the ice-cream cup and eats, listening with pleasure to the Flautist. When the Waiter walks past, Julie signals to him and gives him a coin. The Waiter puts down his tray and takes the coin over to the musician. Julie sees the Flautist thank the Waiter with a slight nod.

INT. JULIE'S FLAT. DAY

It is raining outside. Julie, at the window, is staring at drops trickling down the pane. We can also make out soft shadows of rain on her face. In the room, all the furniture is in place, there is order. She attentively follows one drop of water with her eyes. The drop, hesitating and turning, trickles down. It gets through a gap in the window frame and appears on the sill. It swells. With her finger, Julie helps it trace a route, leads it to the edge of the sill. She takes a glass from the table and stands it under the sill. The drop falls into the glass. Julie smiles as if something important depended on this drop falling into the glass. Maybe she was predicting whether it is possible to live the way she is and the drop has confirmed that possibility.

EXT. JULIE'S HOUSE. DAY

Olivier stands leaning against his car in front of Julie's house, which is now totally deserted. The shutters are closed, grass is appearing between the cracks in the pavement. Olivier is waiting for something, he lights a cigarette. One half of the door opens. A large mattress squeezes through it with difficulty; only after a while do we realize that the mattress is being carried out by the Gardener. He stands it up and looks questioningly at Olivier.

GARDENER

Is this the one?

Olivier looks at the mattress carefully.

OLIVIER

Yes, it is.

It is the same blue mattress on which Olivier and Julie made love.

35

Olivier approaches the Gardener and together they carry the mattress to Olivier's car where the boot is open and back seat lowered. With difficulty, they both place the mattress in the car.

GARDENER
What do you need it for? An old mattress?

OLIVIER
It'd go to waste . . .

Olivier takes 300 francs from his wallet and hands them to the Gardener. He gets into the car and drives away; the mattress sticking out of the boot is tossed up and down on the potholes in the driveway.

INT. HOSPITAL. DAY

The Doctor glances once more at the results of the tests and puts them away in the case file. Julie emerges from behind the screen, buttoning up her blouse.

DOCTOR
Everything's fine physically and you're in good spirits, too. You're on good form. Do you jog?

Julie smiles.

JULIE
I swim. In a month then?

DOCTOR
Maybe two will do . . .

He is interrupted by the phone ringing. He picks up the receiver and listens for a moment to the person on the other end. He then holds the receiver out to Julie.

It's for you.

Julie, surprised and uneasy, holds the receiver to her ear.

JULIE
Hello . . .

Through the receiver she hears the unfamiliar voice of a young man.

MAN'S VOICE
(*off*)

Hello. My name's Antoine . . . you don't know me.

Julie is tense. She replies drily.

JULIE

No, I don't.

MAN'S VOICE
(*off*)

I know. But I'd like to meet you. It's important.

JULIE

Nothing's important.

MAN'S VOICE
(*off*)

It's about an object.

JULIE

What object?

MAN'S VOICE
(*off*)

A chain and cross.

*Julie automatically touches her neck where there is no chain or cross.
For a moment, she says nothing.*

JULIE

All right. Four this afternoon at Wefler's café, Place Clichy.

Julie replaces the receiver, looks at the Doctor.

DOCTOR

Nice man. He was here a couple of times when you were still
in hospital. Then he kept trying to look you up in the phone
book. I agreed that he could ring at this time today. I'm sorry.

JULIE

That's okay.

*She takes a step towards the door, but turns back. She speaks with
determination.*

37

I wanted to thank you for everything. And I wanted to take my file.

Julie holds out her hand; the Doctor, who perhaps would have liked to have asked the reasons for her decision, sees her determination and hands her the file in which he had previously hidden the test results.

INT. WEFLER'S CAFÉ. DAY

Antoine puts a gold chain and cross into Julie's hand. We recognize him; it is the hitchhiker who ran towards the crashed BMW at the beginning of the film. Julie looks at the chain with surprise.

> JULIE
> I'd forgotten I had it . . .

> ANTOINE
> I found it five yards from the car. I took it . . . Then I didn't know how to handle it . . . It was stealing . . .

He smiles a charming, still childish smile. Julie keeps looking at the chain. Then she closes her hand over it, but does not lift her eyes.

Don't you want to know anything? I got there just after . . .

Julie interrupts quite sharply.

38

JULIE

No.

Antoine lowers his head, disheartened by her tone. Julie realizes that she interrupted him a bit too sharply. She touches his wrist.

I'm sorry.

Antoine raises his head. The affair with the chain and perhaps what he saw during the accident must have shaken him up a great deal.

ANTOINE

I was looking for you because of the chain, of course . . . but I wanted you to explain something . . .

JULIE

Yes?

ANTOINE

When I opened the door, your husband was still alive. He said . . .

He pauses. Julie listens attentively.

ANTOINE

He said . . . I don't understand. He said: 'Now try coughing.'

Julie looks at him attentively for a while longer, then starts giggling. She giggles, cannot stop laughing. Antoine looks at her, totally unable to understand her reaction.

JULIE
(*still laughing*)

My husband was telling us a joke. He'd read some book and there was this joke. A woman has a terrible cough. She goes to the doctor and the doctor gives her some pills. 'What sort of pills are these?' the woman asks, swallowing one. 'It's the strongest laxative I know,' the doctor replies. 'Laxative?' The woman's surprised. 'Yes,' the doctor replies. 'Now try coughing.' It made us laugh. Then the car crashed . . .

Antoine smiles at the joke. Julie turns serious.

My husband was one of those people who always likes repeating the punchline.

39

Julie looks at the boy attentively. Then she opens her hand, which she had held clenched around the chain all this time. She lifts it.

You've returned it?

Antoine agrees with a nod. He automatically opens his palm when Julie shifts the chain in his direction.

Now have it as a gift.

Julie lowers the chain until it falls into Antoine's hand. She leaves the café before Antoine has time to react.

INT. SWIMMING POOL. NIGHT

Julie swims the width of the pool with violent strokes. She turns under water and with equal energy swims back. Sprays of water. Tired, she swims to the poolside. She breathes heavily. She submerges her head so as to arrange her hair, shakes it out, grows calmer. She reaches for the side of the pool to get out of the water and freezes. The soundtrack resounds with loud music. Julie heard this music some time ago when she looked at the sheet of paper with a stave of notes jotted on it. She listens to it for a moment, then suddenly submerges her head in the water. The music stops. The water, agitated by Julie's movement, eventually grows calm.

INT./EXT. JULIE'S FLAT. NIGHT

Julie is awoken in the middle of the night by a noise. She sits up, shaken out of her sleep. She realizes that the noise is coming from the street, runs up to the window, pulling on her dressing-gown on the way. There's a fight on the opposite side of the street. It is difficult to see in the dark quite what is going on. It looks like three men against one. The one, in a light-coloured shirt, is strong and agile; he falls and picks himself up several times. When the others finally get to him, they knock him down and kick him mercilessly. The man in the light-coloured shirt huddles up, sheltering his head. Suddenly he springs up and butts one of his opponents in the stomach with his head. The opponent falls. The man, staggering, runs across the street, disappears from Julie's field of vision. Julie opens her window to look down. The three regroup and go after him. They are stopped for a moment by a long lorry driving past. After a while, Julie hears fast, uneven steps on the stairs and a desperate

*thumping on the door below. Nobody opens. The steps approach her
floor. The running man tries to knock on the neighbour's door. Finally
he gets to Julie's door. It is the last floor and his last chance. The
hammering at the door is completely desperate. Julie does not move from
her position near the window. She turns pale. She stops herself from
running to the door and opening. She hears more fast steps on the stairs,
blows, the noise of a body falling and rolling down the stairs. Then
silence. Julie waits a while longer. Only then does she approach the door
and open it.*

INT. STAIRWELL OF JULIE'S FLAT. NIGHT

*There is nobody outside the door. Julie switches on the light in the
corridor – the stairs are empty. She goes to the floor below and looks
down – the stairwell looks as if nothing had happened there. At that
moment, a door slams loudly. Julie quickly turns her head, she knows.
The draught has slammed her front door shut and she, in the middle of
the night, has been left alone on the stairwell wearing nothing but a
flimsy dressing-gown over her naked body.*

*She returns to her own floor with slender hope. Vainly, she pushes the
door, wrenches the door handle, looks for a weak spot in the doorframe.
She closes her eyes, furious with herself. She clenches her fists. She takes
control of herself and starts to act rationally. Through the window on the
stairwell, she can see her terrace but it is quite a distance and the ledge
does not look very solid. Julie opens the window and half goes out, her
leg searches for the ledge which is much lower, and does not find it, so
she goes back inside. She closes the window, the light goes off. She
switches it back on and, having decided to wait until morning, sits on
the stairs. Only now does she realize how cold it is; she huddles up, hugs
herself. The light goes off again. Julie, cold and helpless, her eyes
glistening, now sits in the dark. Tired, she lowers her eyelids and at that
moment we hear a beat of music. Julie immediately opens her eyes; the
music stops. After a while, now consciously trying, she closes her eyes.
The music resounds as before – with a strong beat – and develops. It is
the piece from the music score which we heard before at the swimming
pool. Now it lasts twice as long (about forty seconds).*

*We do not know how long she has been sitting there when the light on
the stairwell goes on again. The music stops immediately. Julie opens*

41

her eyes, unconscious, not quite knowing at first where she is and what she is doing there. She hears footsteps approaching from below. She sees a young woman open the door to her flat on the floor below. She is called Lucille. Before going into her flat, Lucille softly scratches her finger against her neighbour's door and disappears. Julie does not quite understand this scratching. The light goes off. The door which Lucille scratched opens, and the mystery is explained. The Neighbour, trying not to make a noise, a shirt thrown over his trousers, slips through the girl's door. She has obviously left the door open because he goes in without difficulty. Julie smiles, it is obvious. She gets up and leans over the bannister. She goes down a few steps, but quickly has to return to her old spot because Lucille's door opens and the Neighbour appears on the stairwell. Sensing somebody's eyes on him or hearing a rustling, the Neighbour turns on the light and looks up, sees Julie sitting on the stairs.

NEIGHBOUR

Hello . . .

JULIE

Hello.

The Neighbour opens the door to his flat. Through a gap below, a large, beautiful, well-tended cat emerges.

NEIGHBOUR

Locked out?

Julie nods. The Neighbour tries to talk quietly.

I forgot my keys once. Sat it out on the stairs till morning, too. You don't want to wake the caretaker?

JULIE

No.

NEIGHBOUR

My wife's asleep. A cannon wouldn't wake her . . . Would you like to sit it out at my place? Or sleep?

She does not know why, but somehow Julie senses some ambiguity in his proposal.

JULIE

Thanks, I'll sit here.

The Neighbour calls his cat which, tail held taut and high, disappears back into the flat. He winks knowingly to Julie and closes the door. Julie smiles bitterly to herself. The Neighbour's door opens again. He is carrying a blanket and mug of tea.

NEIGHBOUR

At least have something to drink. It's hot.

He hands her the blanket and mug.

You can give them back to me tomorrow.

He winks again, goes down and disappears into his flat. Julie wraps herself in the blanket and brings the mug of tea to her lips. She smells the blanket, frowns and pushes it away from her face.

EXT. PARIS SUBURBS. DAY

Julie in a park. She breathes the sharp air in deeply, with obvious pleasure. She closes her eyes, absorbing the sun. Perhaps she wants to hear the music which sometimes resounds in her thoughts, but this time there is complete silence. Julie does not notice the neatly dressed Old Woman approaching a green, metal container for recycling glass with a large glass bottle in her hand. The Old Woman gets up on her toes and tries to put the bottle into the container. She is too old and too humpbacked to reach. She jumps up awkwardly, in vain. The bottle is stuck halfway through the rubber collar of the container. The Old Woman leaves. Julie, inclined a little unnaturally towards the sun, with a slight smile on her face, does not open her eyes. She shakes her head, wakes from her sunny trance. She stretches, gets up.

EXT. STREETS OF PARIS SUBURBS. DAY

Julie walks in the direction of her flat with pleasure, adapting her pace to the rhythm of the Flautist's music as she passes him. Without changing her pace, she disappears in the gate of her building. The Flautist does not pay any attention to Julie; he continues playing. He looks in the direction of the café. At the table where Julie usually sits, now sits Olivier. He has a glass of wine in his hand. The Waiter brings another glass which has obviously been ordered earlier. Olivier indicates the Flautist to him. The Waiter shrugs, approaches the Flautist, hands him the glass.

INT. JULIE'S FLAT. DAY

Julie rearranges the furniture in her flat. What used to be the large room is now her bedroom. She eases the bed through the narrow doorway. She squeezes between the upturned bed and the doorway and from the other side, using all her strength, she pushes the bed with her legs; it falls to the floor with a thud. The doorbell rings. Julie straightens herself, she is not expecting anyone. She opens. A pleasant forty-year-old woman with the face of a teacher stands in the doorway. She is holding some documents in her hands. It is the Neighbour's Wife. Julie smiles, opens the door wider.

> JULIE
> I'm sorry about the noise. I've almost finished.

> NEIGHBOUR'S WIFE
> I didn't hear anything . . . May I?

She goes in, looks around at the mess. She spreads her papers out on the table, which is standing askew, after first wiping it with her hand, uncertain of whether it is clean.

> (*kindheartedly*)
> I heard you got locked out last week?

> JULIE
> Yes. Your husband lent me a blanket. I was sitting on the stairs.

> NEIGHBOUR'S WIFE
> I wanted to ask you to sign this.

Julie goes up to the table and looks through the papers. Surprised, she looks up.

> JULIE
> What is it?

NEIGHBOUR'S WIFE
Everyone's signed already. We don't want women who
entertain men living in our building. The young person below
you . . .

Julie gathers up the papers and hands them to the Neighbour's Wife.

JULIE
I'm sorry. I don't want to get involved.

NEIGHBOUR'S WIFE
She's a whore.

Julie raises her voice a little, although she remains calm.

JULIE
That's nothing to do with me.

*The Neighbour's Wife looks at her coldly. Julie, not worried by it, leans
over the bed and drags it to the corner of the room. The Neighbour's
Wife, furious, impulsively follows her, then suddenly leaves the flat.
Julie, tired with the effort, leans against the bed and quietly giggles.*

EXT. PARIS SUBURBS. DUSK

*Julie returns home with her shopping. She turns the corner and does not
hear the usual flute music. She slows down, stops. On the pavement by
the wall where he usually sits and plays, lies the Flautist, beside him a
closed flute-case. Julie approaches and stands over him. Obviously
drunk, a thin stream of spittle trickles down his chin. With her foot,
Julie pushes the flute-case closer to his head. The Flautist wakes up and,
not recognizing Julie, stares at her. Julie pushes the case even closer to
his head. The Flautist lifts his head and, content, settles it on the case.
He murmurs something. Julie cannot understand the words. She leans
over.*

JULIE
Did you say something?

FLAUTIST
You always gotta keep something.

JULIE
I don't understand.

The Flautist takes a deep breath and falls asleep. Julie gets up and walks away without looking. Round the corner she shrugs, feeling that – maybe – she has done something foolish.

INT. JULIE'S FLAT. DAY

Julie under the shower. She surrenders herself to the strong jet of water. She turns the water off and for a moment longer stands motionless, holding her head back with pleasure, feeling the drops of water trickle from her hair down her back.

Wrapped in a towel, her hair still wet, Julie chooses a pair of knickers from her drawer. She ponders over the colour of the tiny pants. She opens another drawer and, under the light, examines various types of tights.

Dressed in jeans with a blouse thrown over her, she pours herself a full cup of coffee. These daily activities which she can now perform exactly as she pleases give her satisfaction. The doorbell, too, gives her pleasure. She opens the door and there stands Lucille. She is holding a small bunch of flowers in her hand. She presents it to Julie.

LUCILLE

Thanks.

Julie takes the flowers, uncertain of whether she is doing the right thing.

JULIE

What for?

Lucille walks in without embarrassment.

LUCILLE

I'm staying. They needed everyone's signature to kick me
out. So I'm staying. It's nice here . . .

*She looks around the flat which Julie has managed to tidy up. She stops
in the middle of the room. She looks up, smiles.*

I had a lamp like that when I was little. I'd stand under it and
stretch out my hand . . .

She pauses. Julie looks at her with curiosity.

I dreamt of jumping up and touching it. Then I grew up and
forgot all about it . . .

She stretches her arms up and touches the lamp with her palms.

*Lucille, just as informally as she had walked in, speaks familiarly to
Julie.*

Where did you get it from?

JULIE

I just got it.

LUCILLE

Is it a souvenir?

Julie nods. Lucille submits easily.

You live alone?

JULIE

Yes.

LUCILLE

I couldn't stand one night alone.

47

She looks at Julie closely.

> Something must have happened. You're not the type
> somebody dumps . . .

Julie does not answer.

> Sorry. I talk too much.

She goes up to the window and looks down.

> Poor guy.

JULIE

Who?

LUCILLE

He was asleep last night when I came home. Now he's gone,
but his flute's still there.

*Julie goes up to her. She is right, the Flautist is not there but his small
flute-case lies by the wall.*

EXT. PARIS SUBURBS. DAY

*Julie leaves the building. She approaches the flute-case. It is still early in
the morning, the traffic quieter than in the middle of the day. She leans
over, opens the case. Inside lies the untouched flute and inside the lid is
attached a small card with a name, address and telephone number. Julie
picks up the case and goes to the nearest telephone box with it. Holding
up the open case so as to see the number, she punches out the successive
digits. A woman's voice answers.*

JULIE

Is that 43 07 92 74?

WOMAN'S VOICE
(*off*)

Yes.

JULIE

I found this number in a flute-case . . .

WOMAN'S VOICE
(*off*)

That's right.

JULIE

Somebody left it in the street.

WOMAN'S VOICE
(*off*)

That somebody got drunk. And forgot his instrument. It happens. He came home in the early hours and is now sleeping next to me. Maybe he slept next to you last night . . .

JULIE

No. I found the flute in the street. That is . . .

WOMAN'S VOICE
(*off*)

I know where he plays. Could you look after it?

JULIE

No. I'll put it back. I haven't got time.

WOMAN'S VOICE
(*off*)

I'll come and get it. Thanks.

Julie replaces the receiver. She closes the case and goes back to the pavement with it. She puts it back where she found it and, walking briskly, returns home. At the gate, she looks back. Surprised, she sees that the case has disappeared. Among other people in the street she notices a tall, unshaven Guy who, walking at a leisurely pace, is holding his jacket as if he were hiding something. Julie, running now and again, quickly catches up with him. At the corner of the round plaza, she grabs him by the sleeve of his jacket. The Guy does not slow down. Julie says quietly.

JULIE

You stole the flute.

The Guy turns around surprised. It looks as if he does not know what she is talking about. Julie repeats with determination, louder.

You stole the flute!

She starts tugging at his sleeve. Several people stop near by. The Guy smiles sweetly and easily frees himself from Julie's grasp.

GUY

I haven't stolen anything.

He reaches under his jacket, takes out the case, hands it over to Julie and calmly, slowly walks away. Julie opens the case, the flute is inside. Once again Julie takes it back to its place by the building. For a while, she stands beside it and then, looking behind, sits at the table of her street café. The Waiter appears.

WAITER

The usual?

JULIE

No. Only coffee. I haven't had time for a coffee.

She leans out so as not to take her eyes off the case for a single moment but nothing happens – the case lies peacefully, people walk by. Suddenly Julie hears her name spoken out loud. She turns around. Two paces away from her stands Olivier. Julie looks at him, completely taken aback. Olivier looks at her tensely. The Waiter approaches, places the coffee in front of Julie. Olivier raises his hand.

OLIVIER

Coffee, too.

Without waiting for an invitation, or rather so as to show the Waiter where he's going to have his coffee, he sits opposite Julie. The Waiter nods, walks away.

I've been looking for you . . .

JULIE

And?

Olivier smiles.

OLIVIER

I've found you.

JULIE

No one knows where I live.

OLIVIER

No one. It took a couple of months, then by chance it turned
out to be very simple. My cleaning lady's daughter's seen you
in the area. I've been coming here for three days . . . I wasn't
far when you caught the thief.

JULIE

You're spying on me.

OLIVIER

No. I miss you.

JULIE

Oh, God . . .

OLIVIER

Yes.

*The conversation dies for a while. Julie lowers her eyes; Olivier, on the
contrary, fixes his eyes on her face. The Waiter puts Olivier's coffee
down, but this doesn't change anything; it is as if neither of them has
noticed.*

You ran away?

Julie does not answer.

Tell me . . . Did you run away from me?

*Julie, with a little smile, slowly shakes her head. Olivier turns silent.
Julie notices a large car stop by the kerb near the flute-case. The Flautist
clambers out of the back seat. A well-dressed woman lets him by, getting
out for a moment herself. The car drives away and the Flautist takes the
instrument out of its case, sits and begins to play his fine melody.
Following Julie's eyes, Olivier, too, watches the scene.*

JULIE

Do you hear what he's playing?

Olivier listens carefully. His face brightens up.

OLIVIER

It sounds a bit like . . .

JULIE

Exactly.

Both of them listen to the music of the flute for a while. Olivier gazes at Julie all the time.

OLIVIER

That time during the night . . . you thought I was asleep. But I wasn't. I heard what you said.

JULIE

Good. Now you know.

Olivier looks at her with despair in his eyes.

OLIVIER

I've seen you. Maybe that'll do for now. I'll try.

He gets up. He has not touched his coffee. He takes out some change and leaves it on the table. He leaves, gets into his car parked close by and drives away. Driving past Julie, he raises his hand in goodbye and Julie does the same. With unexpected greediness she drinks her coffee and immediately afterwards drinks Olivier's, both cold by now. She grimaces. She gets up from the table and leaves the café. She passes the Flautist, remembers something, goes back, leans over him. The Flautist calmly continues his music to the end of the phrase, ignoring Julie's presence. When he has finished the phrase, he tears the flute away from his lips.

JULIE

You fell asleep here yesterday . . .

The Flautist nods, pleased.

I leant over you.

FLAUTIST

I can't remember.

Considering the conversation finished, he brings the flute to his lips.

JULIE

Where do you know that from? The music?

FLAUTIST

I make up lots of things. I like playing.

*Not waiting for a response, he starts playing. Julie listens a while
longer, squatting down beside him. She takes out a coin from her
trouser pocket and drops it into the case. The Flautist gravely thanks
her with a bow.*

INT. JULIE'S FLAT. DUSK

*Julie turns the light on in the hall of her flat and freezes mid-movement
with a broken scream. She has caught sight of a mouse in the corner of
the hall. The mouse is sitting strangely huddled against the wall,
motionless. Julie, too, for a moment stands paralysed. She does not
know what to do, so she moves a little, convinced that the mouse will
run away, but the mouse remains motionless. She takes a step forward,
but the mouse only looks at her with completely motionless eyes. She goes
out into the kitchen and finds a long broom. She returns, stands over the
mouse and raises the broom. She closes her eyes before striking, but opens
them at the last moment – she wants to be sure of her aim. She notices,
with amazement, something she had not noticed before. She leans over
and retreats, lowering the broom. She realizes now that the mouse has a
very good reason for not moving. She is giving birth. Julie stands utterly
fascinated. Not long afterwards several tiny mice appear next to the
mouse – it looks like a miracle and Julie watches it as if it were. Slowly,
very softly, she backs out of the hall. Just as softly, she closes the door.
Once in the room, she leans back against the door and listens. She smiles
a strange, pained smile.*

INT. OLIVIER'S FLAT. DUSK

*Olivier turns to the telephone with a sudden decision. He quickly
punches out a number. For a long time nobody picks up the phone.
Finally a man's voice answers.*

OLIVIER

It's Olivier. Not disturbing you, am I?

The man's voice is a bit sleepy.

> MAN'S VOICE
> (*off*)

You are a bit.

> OLIVIER

I'm sorry. I thought I'd try to finish it. Phone them if you would. It's not too late, I hope.

> MAN'S VOICE
> (*off*)

I don't think so. They gave us till yesterday. I'm glad you've decided. Good. I'll give them a buzz.

Olivier replaces the receiver.

INT. JULIE'S FLAT. NIGHT

Julie cannot sleep. Maybe affected by what she had seen that evening or perhaps worried that something will have to be done about it, she is lying with her head inclined to one side. She gazes somewhere into the distance, into space. Her eyes focus when she hears the mouse scratching as it moves around in the hall; she sees its shadow in the opening of the door. She backs away a bit, thinking that the mouse is getting through the opening into the room. She is not sure whether it has slipped into the kitchen. No doubt it has because she thinks she sees it going back to the hall. After a while, when everything grows quiet, her gaze melts into the distance again.

INT. JULIE'S FLAT. DAY

In the kitchen, Julie cuts several pieces of cheese, then, after some thought, adds a piece of sausage. She makes her way towards the door leading to the hall, but stops just in front of it, thinks for a moment and returns to the kitchen. She pours herself a mug of coffee and for some time, agitated, paces around the flat with it. Once again she stops in front of the hall door. We can see by her expression that she is making a decision. She puts the mug of coffee down and slips on her jacket.

INT. ESTATE AGENTS. DAY

The Proprietor is just as charming and well dressed as he was the first time. He has a small plaster on his right cheek.

PROPRIETOR
(*surprised*)
Aren't you happy with your flat?

JULIE
On the contrary. I'd like to change it for another one just like it.

The Proprietor leans over his computer, presses the keys. He smiles.

PROPRIETOR
I think I can find you one. But it'll take some time.

JULIE
How long?

PROPRIETOR
Two or three months.

Julie studies him.

JULIE
You've cut yourself shaving.

The Proprietor touches the plaster on his cheek. He pulls it off, grimacing a bit.

PROPRIETOR
The cat scratched me.

INT. STAIRWELL OF JULIE'S FLAT. DAY

Julie energetically knocks on one of the doors of her stairwell. She knocks again. The door opens and the Neighbour appears. He is astonished and uneasy for a moment, but smiles. He makes a gesture of invitation.

NEIGHBOUR
I'm glad to see you. Come in . . .

Julie does not move from the threshold.

JULIE
I've got a favour to ask.

NEIGHBOUR

Come on in. My wife's gone out . . .

JULIE

Can you lend me your cat?

NEIGHBOUR

I beg your pardon?

JULIE

Your cat.

The Neighbour scrutinizes her, uncertain as to whether she is joking. Julie has obviously decided.

I need a cat. For a couple of days.

NEIGHBOUR

He's not been neutered and is aggressive. I'm not sure he likes you.

JULIE

It doesn't matter.

The Neighbour nods and, with an expression of 'as you like', goes into his flat. He returns with the cat under his arm. He hands it over to Julie and closes the door. Julie, the cat under her arm, climbs up to her floor. She stops at the door. The cat watches her with hostility. Julie unlocks the door to her flat, only half opens it and pushes the cat inside. Then she abruptly slams the door and, her heels resounding against the floor, quickly runs down the stairs.

INT. SWIMMING POOL. DAY

Julie swims to the end of the pool, turns and moves off again. She is swimming very fast, is already tired. She swims fifty metres, wants to turn but notices somebody at the poolside. She grabs the edge. Just by the edge of the pool, splashed with streams of water, squats Lucille. She wipes the drops of water from her face.

JULIE

What're you doing here?

LUCILLE

I saw you from the bus. You were running like crazy . . .
Breathless, there was a film like that. That's just how you
were running.

JULIE

I saw it.

LUCILLE

Are you crying?

JULIE

It's the water.

*She wants to change the subject, she is finding it difficult to hold back
the tears. Just above her are Lucille's legs. She looks at them.*

You don't wear knickers?

LUCILLE

Never.

*She smiles pleasantly. Julie also tries to smile and that brings back the
tears. She hides her face in her hands. Lucille takes her hand and helps
her climb out. She puts her arms around her, completely wet, hugs her.
They remain like that for a while.*

JULIE

I borrowed the neighbour's cat to eat the mice. It had
babies . . .

LUCILLE

It's normal, Julie. You're afraid to go back?

Julie nods.

Give me the keys. I'll go and clear up.

*Julie approaches the bench at the poolside and takes out a key from the
trousers lying there.*

I'll wait for you at my place.

*She leaves. Julie approaches the edge of the pool. She wants to dive in
and lifts her arms. At that moment dozens of little girls dressed in white*

57

bathing suits run in. Laughing, screaming, they jump into the pool.
Julie lowers her arms, goes back and sits on the bench beside her clothes.

INT. OLIVIER'S FLAT. DUSK

Olivier places ten francs in the palm of an elderly man wearing a
motorbike helmet and, holding a very large, stiff envelope, closes the
door behind him. He approaches a table full of papers. He clears
everything, places the telephone on a small stool. Celebrating the
moment, he carefully cuts the edge of the envelope with a pair of scissors
and pulls out some large music scores. He spreads them out on the table,
leans over. He is looking at them for the first time. They are the same
scores as the ones which Julie threw into the rubbish truck after collecting
them from the Copyist. He carefully examines the scores and the
corrections made in a blue felt-tip pen which accompany practically
every line. He goes back to the first page. He picks it up and goes to the
piano. The first few bars on the keyboard.

EXT. SMALL RAILWAY STATION NEAR PARIS. DAY

A suburban train stops at the station. The only person getting off is
Julie. The train pulls away and Julie, obviously knowing her way,

walks along a tree-lined alley in the direction of a block of buildings. She passes the gate, then the front door and approaches a fine building on the side of a well-kept park. She nears the open window of one of the rooms. She stands at the window and smiles.

> JULIE

Mum . . .

INT. ROOM IN A REST-HOME. DAY

An old woman in a comfortable armchair studies Julie with effort. It is Julie's Mother. Maybe it is because of the light – Julie is standing with the sun behind her – that the old woman cannot recognize her. Her face suddenly brightens up.

> MOTHER

Marie-France . . .

> JULIE

No, Mum. It's me, Julie.

> MOTHER

Julie . . . Come closer.

Julie disappears from the bright window-frame; her Mother tries to concentrate. Her face shows that she is obviously struggling with her memory, with returning to reality. Julie appears in the doorway. She snuggles up to her Mother who embraces her warmly without getting up from the armchair.

They told me you were dead.

She studies Julie.

You look well. Young.

JULIE

Yes, Mum.

MOTHER

Very young. You were always younger than me, but now you look thirty . . . When we were little . . .

JULIE

I'm not your sister, Mum. I'm your daughter. I'm thirty-four.

MOTHER

I know, I know. I'm only joking. I'm fine. I've got everything here. I'm watching . . .

She indicates the TV, which is turned on. Colourfully dressed men and women jump from a high bridge and then, tied by a bungee cord, swing over an abyss. Julie's Mother watches with great interest.

They show you the whole world.

She turns away from the TV with regret.

Do you watch, too?

JULIE

No.

MOTHER

That's what I thought. Do you want to tell me something? About your husband, your home, the children. Or about yourself?

JULIE

My husband and daughter . . . are dead. I haven't got a
home.

MOTHER

Yes, they told me. Poor Marie-France . . .

She extends her arm and strokes Julie's hair. Julie submits to this caress.
After a short moment of concentration, the old woman, still stroking her
daughter's head, raises her eyes beyond Julie, towards the TV. Julie
realizes that her Mother is not present; maybe that is why she starts
talking.

JULIE

I was happy, Mum. I loved them. They loved me, too. I
didn't rebel . . . That's how it would've been for the rest of
my life. But what happened happened and they're not here
any more. I . . . Are you listening, Mum?

Her Mother does not take her eyes off the TV.

MOTHER

I'm listening, Marie-France.

JULIE

I realized that, since that's happened, I'll only do what I want
to now. Nothing. I don't want any memories or things, no
friends, love or ties . . . They're all a trap . . .

When Julie starts saying she does not want anything, her Mother frowns
and turns her eyes away from the TV. Focused, she now studies her
daughter.

MOTHER

Do you have any money, my child? To get by?

JULIE

I do, Mum.

MOTHER

That's important. You can't give up everything.

JULIE

Yes.

Her Mother, reassured, nods and immediately loses interest in Julie. On TV another daredevil is getting ready to jump. With a movement of her head Julie's Mother helps him make the decision and watches the fall with pleasure.

Mum . . .

MOTHER

Yes?

JULIE

Was I scared of mice? When I was little?

MOTHER

No, you weren't. It was Julie who was scared.

JULIE

I'm scared now.

MOTHER

They've finished.

On TV, the picture of a young man swinging upside down on a bungee cord slowly darkens.

EXT. PARIS SUBURBS. DAY

Julie emerges around the corner of her street. The Flautist is at his spot, playing. Everything is as it should be. Julie walks along lightly, listening to the fine voice of the flute, amused. She passes the Flautist, walks away, swinging her handbag and swaying to the rhythm of the music, if the music has rhythm. The Flautist watches Julie walking away and, seeing her amusement – as an experiment – suddenly breaks off. Julie catches on and stops mid-step. She is now standing with her back to the Flautist, motionless.

FLAUTIST

Excuse me!

Julie turns around.

You want to get to know me?

JULIE

What do you have in mind?

FLAUTIST

I don't know. Talk. Have dinner. Go to bed.

JULIE

No.

Completely undeterred by her refusal, the Flautist starts to play again. Julie moves off to the sound of the music, swinging her bag.

INT. JULIE'S FLAT. NIGHT

Julie looks at her face in the mirror. She tilts her head, tries a smile, brings her hands to her lips and pulls at them. She smiles at these efforts, and this comes naturally. The ringing telephone does not spoil her good mood.

JULIE

Hello?

LUCILLE
(*off*)

It's Lucille. Julie, I need a favour. Grab a taxi and come here. I'll pay you back.

JULIE

Now? It's ten at night.

LUCILLE
(*off*)

Now. You've got twenty-five minutes to get here. It's important.

JULIE

I can't.

LUCILLE
(*off*)

I beg you. I've never asked for anything. I have to now. Please come.

> JULIE

Where is it?

> LUCILLE
> (*off*)

Seven rue Frochot. It's a little street off the Pigalle. Third gate on the left, then it's the first door on the right. There's a buzzer. Ring and say it's for me. Will you come?

Julie thinks for a moment before answering.

EXT. NEAR PLACE PIGALLE. NIGHT

Julie walks quickly from the Place Pigalle. It is busy. She squeezes through, counts the gates. She enters the third one on the left, glancing at her watch. The doorway is hideous and stinks. She presses the buzzer, looking at her watch.

> MAN'S VOICE
> (*on the intercom, off*)

Yes?

> JULIE

I've come to see Lucille.

There is a twang; the lock is released.

INT. CABARET LIVE-SHOW. NIGHT

Julie slams the door. Semi-darkness inside. Further inside, from the wings, we see a small stage revolving on which two naked girls are playing with plastic imitations of male genitals. Julie looks on for a moment, but Lucille is not there. A few more people are also milling around inside, among them a Boy in briefs. She notices the half-naked Lucille sitting with her back to her by a small bar with an espresso machine. She approaches her. Lucille is resting her head on one hand, holding a whisky glass in the other. Her eyes are red and she is wiping her nose with a large handkerchief.

> LUCILLE

You came . . .

JULIE

Yes.

LUCILLE

I'm sorry.

She hides her face in her hands again. Julie sits down opposite her.

LUCILLE

Sorry.

With one hand she reaches for a clean glass and pours some whisky. She hands it to Julie. For a while, Lucille's shoulders continue to tremble, and then she suddenly pulls the handkerchief away from her face and smiles. She is a bit drunk.

You're not angry, are you?

Julie shakes her head. Lucille holds her glass out to her and they both take a sip. The Boy in briefs comes and stands over Lucille.

BOY

We're on in five minutes. Give us a hand.

Lucille puts her hand on his briefs. She leans over to Julie.

LUCILLE

I got undressed in the dressing-room and came here for a drink. Just by chance I glanced at the audience. And right in the middle of the front row was my father.

The Boy stops Lucille's hand.

BOY

Thanks.

The Boy goes away, Lucille continues talking without stopping.

LUCILLE

He was tired and kept dozing off, but he kept staring at the ass of the girl on stage. That lout . . .

She indicates a Big Man standing near the stage.

Son of a bitch . . . he said he doesn't care. You pay, you've got a right to watch. Who likes me? I thought. I was completely desperate. I phoned you . . .

65

> **JULIE**
>
> What happened to him?

> **LUCILLE**
>
> Ten minutes ago, he looked at his watch and left. I realized
> . . . the last train home to Montpellier is at eleven-fifteen.

She smiles brightly, a little childishly.

> **JULIE**
>
> Why do you do this, Lucille?

> **LUCILLE**
>
> Because I like it.

Julie also smiles a little. What Lucille says sounds genuine.

> I think that everybody likes it really. Julie . . . you saved my
> life.

> **JULIE**
>
> I didn't do anything.

> **LUCILLE**
>
> You came. I asked you and you came. It comes to the same
> thing.

> **JULIE**
>
> No. I didn't . . .

> **LUCILLE**
>
> Julie . . .

Lucille is looking a little to the side. Something has caught her attention.

> Isn't that you?

*Julie turns around. Above the audience there is a window to the sound
cabin. The guy sitting there, bored of what he sees on stage every day, is
watching TV. Julie sees on screen what Lucille had seen a moment
earlier – herself in a still photograph. She's standing on a beach,
embracing her husband Patrick in some southern country.*

> **JULIE**
>
> It's me . . .

The camera slowly zooms in on Patrick's face. Julie watches the TV, gets up, moves closer, almost to the stage itself. She does not pay any attention to Lucille who, together with the Boy in briefs, is on stage beginning her performance. Because of the glass windows of the sound cabin and the music coming through the loudspeakers, Julie does not hear the soundtrack of the broadcast.

On TV, Ms Gaudry, the female Journalist who spoke to Julie in the hospital, is talking to Olivier. Olivier is showing her large music scores and, for a moment, the camera reveals a close-up of the blue marks made with a felt-tip pen. Julie watches this, agitated. Olivier calmly points to individual notes or groups of notes and taps his finger against the blue marks. During this conversation still photographs of Patrick in various situations are cut in: Patrick writing at his desk; laughing, with a glass in his hand; entering the opera or philharmonic in a dinner jacket with Julie at his side; during an orchestra rehearsal; receiving some state award. There are private photographs of Patrick and Julie. Usually Olivier is standing next to them. There are two photographs of Julie turning her back, with a blanket and book under her arm on the hospital terrace. Then three or four photographs, obviously from a series, are briefly shown in which Patrick appears with a young, fair-haired girl.

Judging by her expression, Julie has never seen these photographs.

The camera returns to the studio and Olivier, showing more scores of music, again explains something to the Journalist. The Journalist appears convinced, turns to the camera and now speaks directly to the viewers, obviously bidding them goodbye. Credits appear against the wide shot of the studio.

Julie turns. Right next to her stands the Big Man. He is watching Lucille's and the Boy's performance – the Boy is no longer wearing briefs – with pleasure.

JULIE
Excuse me . . . is there a phone here?

The Big Man points behind him. Beside the door is a little table with a telephone on it. Julie quickly goes to it. She chucks everything out of her bag, flicks through the pages of her address book – all of them are blank. She slams the book shut, reaches for the receiver and punches out directory enquiries. She waits impatiently, tapping the edge of the table with her new address book. Finally a girl answers.

Could you please give me the number of Ms Gaudry.

GIRL
(*off*)

One moment, please.

Julie walks around with the telephone as far as the length of the cable lets her. She pays no attention to the way Lucille's situation on stage is developing.

(*off*)
Ms Gaudry's first name?

JULIE
I think it's Annette . . . or Agnes. No, it's Annette.

GIRL
(*off*)

And address?

JULIE
I don't know.

GIRL
(*off*)

I've got a Ms Annette Gaudry. But she's ex-directory.

JULIE
I'm her sister. I'm calling from the station, I've just arrived. I forgot my address book and she was supposed to come and pick me up and she's not here . . .

The Girl interrupts her.

GIRL
(*off*)

The number's ex-directory. I'm not allowed to give it to you.

JULIE
Could you call her and ask her to call me?

She picks up the telephone, glances at the number.

68

My number is 48 34 . . .

The Girl interrupts her again.

GIRL
(off)
There's no number beginning with 48 in any of the public phones at any station.

We hear the girl replace the receiver.

JULIE
True.

She stands holding the receiver for a moment longer, then softly replaces it. Lucille, snuggled up to the Boy, is returning from the stage. She delicately touches his face, the Boy kisses her hair. Lucille lets him go and smiles at Julie.

LUCILLE
Jesus, that was good, Julie. It was real good today . . .

JULIE
You knew?

LUCILLE
What?

JULIE
That the programme was going to be on. Is that why you asked me to come here?

Lucille looks at her calmly. She carries on smiling.

Did you know?

Lucille, still smiling, shakes her head. She did not know.

EXT. STREET IN FRONT OF THE COPYIST'S FLAT. NIGHT

A taxi stops in front of the Copyist's flat. Julie gets out of the car without paying and asks the driver to wait for her. She swears quietly as she passes the gate.

JULIE
Shit . . .

She doesn't know the code for the obviously newly fitted lock. She hears footsteps on the staircase and the door opens. An enormous dog emerges, followed by its Owner, who can barely keep up. Julie watches them and, before the door closes, slips inside.

INT. COPYIST'S FLAT. NIGHT

Evidently the Copyist was already in bed. And not alone at that – the Copyist's Boyfriend peers from the bedroom door, curious as to the guest. He retreats, embarrassed by Julie's look. He is young and cheerful and his head immediately reappears at the door.

> JULIE
> I'm sorry.

The Copyist smiles. She searches through her papers, turns over scores, rummages through drawers.

> COPYIST
> You're not disturbing me at all. Where did I put it? A pale green business card.

> JULIE
> (*completely out of the blue*)
> Did you watch TV tonight?

The Boy bursts out laughing, the Copyist too. Her dressing-gown half opens to reveal a lovely, generous bust.

> COPYIST
> No, no way. Ah, here it is . . .

Among the mess she finally finds the pale green business card. She hands it to Julie.

> Her number at home and at work.

Julie wants to copy the numbers, but the Copyist waves her hand; she is not going to need the card. She approaches Julie still closer.

> Why do you want her number?

> JULIE
> Tonight on TV . . .

Julie thinks for a moment. The Copyist watches her, uneasy.

Her programme was on tonight. They showed the score which I took from you.

The Copyist lowers her eyes.

> COPYIST
After the accident . . . not everything was sure . . . I made a copy. I realized you'd destroy it. I kept a copy and sent it to Strasbourg . . .

> JULIE
What for?

> COPYIST
The music's beautiful. You can't destroy things like that.

Julie unexpectedly touches her gently on the shoulder. The Copyist raises her eyes and sees that Julie has brightened up.

You said we wouldn't see each other again . . .

> JULIE
Exactly.

With a movement of her head, the Copyist discreetly gestures in her Boyfriend's direction. She asks in a whisper.

> COPYIST
Do you like him?

Julie looks him over carefully. The Boyfriend looks amiable, he's obviously younger than the Copyist.

> JULIE
Yes.

The Copyist lowers her whisper even more.

> COPYIST
I love him.

EXT. STREET IN FRONT OF THE COPYIST'S FLAT. NIGHT

Julie runs past the gate and gets into the waiting taxi.

INT. JULIE'S FLAT. NIGHT

Julie, holding the pale green card in her hand, quickly taps out a number. The Journalist's voice answers after the first ring.

JOURNALIST
(*off*)
Hello, this is 42 23 07 79. I'm not at home at the moment. Please leave a message after the tone and I'll get back to you as soon as I can.

We hear a short, electronic tone. Julie makes a move to replace the receiver, but at the last moment brings it up to her ear again.

JULIE
This is Julie, Patrick's wife. I hope you remember me. Please . . .

At that moment the Journalist herself answers.

JOURNALIST
(*off*)
Hello . . .

We hear the answering machine being switched off.

JULIE
Hello.

JOURNALIST
(*off*)
I'm here. I wasn't answering the phone. Is that you, Julie?

JULIE
Yes.

JOURNALIST
(*off*)
Did you see the programme?

JULIE
Yes.

JOURNALIST
(*off*)

Did you like it?

JULIE

I didn't hear anything. I only saw . . .

JOURNALIST
(*off*)

Doesn't your TV work?

JULIE

I don't have one. I saw . . . never mind. Can you tell me what it's all about? What was it?

JOURNALIST
(*off*)

A programme about Patrick in which you didn't want to take part. And about the concert that doesn't exist.

JULIE

And the score? Where did you get the score from?

JOURNALIST
(*off*)

Olivier. He's going to finish the concert. He came to the studio with the score, photographs, materials . . .

Julie does not answer for a moment.

Are you there?

JULIE

Yes, I am.

JOURNALIST
(*off*)

I've had very good feedback so far. I can send you a video when you get your TV mended.

JULIE

Thanks.

We hear a rustling of papers at the other end of the line.

> JOURNALIST
> (*off*)
>
> I've just got a pen. I haven't got your address.

> JULIE
>
> Thanks. I don't need the video. Goodnight.

> JOURNALIST
> (*off*)
>
> As you wish. Goodnight.

Julie replaces the receiver. Then she picks it up and slams the phone as hard as she can.

EXT. PARIS SUBURBS. DAY

Julie approaches the Waiter in her regular café.

She has not been here since her meeting with Olivier, so the Waiter greets her more effusively than usual. Julie immediately gets to the point.

> JULIE
>
> That guy I had coffee with hasn't been here by any chance, has he? You remember?

The Waiter nods, he remembers.

> WAITER
>
> Yes, he has. Three days ago. He sat for about an hour. He was waiting for you.

> JULIE
>
> If he comes today . . . Tell him I've gone to look for him.

EXT. NEIGHBOURHOOD NEAR OLIVIER'S FLAT. DAY

Julie emerges from the metro exit. With a sure, brisk step she crosses the square, checks the name of the street and, running a little, glancing at the ascending numbers, she makes her way along the pavement. The street forms a broad crescent at this point. Julie notices something which makes her stop for a while. From a house on the opposite side of the crescent Olivier emerges. He doesn't notice Julie. He goes up to his car, removes some leaflets from behind the windscreen wiper and throws them on the ground. Julie stands at the kerb and holds her hands up to her mouth.

JULIE

Olivier! *Olivier!*

Olivier does not hear, there is the usual traffic; a fire-engine with its siren screaming passes by. Julie runs in Olivier's direction. She has still got about a hundred yards to go. Olivier gets into his car, slams the door. He fastens his seat-belt, turns the engine on and, slowly reversing, moves out from his tight parking space. Julie still has twenty yards to go. She runs faster, shouts again as she runs.

JULIE

Olivier!

Olivier, of course, does not hear; his window is closed. Another car is in his lane so he has to stop for a moment. Then he moves and at that moment Julie catches up with the car. Tired from running, she thumps the rear window and boot with all her might. Olivier, hearing the thumps, brakes sharply. Julie runs into the braking car and lies half sprawled across the boot. Olivier gets out, helps her up. Julie straightens herself. She is fine, only breathless after running.

OLIVIER

Sorry, I didn't see you . . .

JULIE

You can't do that.

OLIVIER

I didn't see you. I simply moved off . . .

Julie interrupts him abruptly.

JULIE

I'm not talking about the car. I'm talking about the concert. You want to finish Patrick's concert.

OLIVIER

I thought I could try . . . Do you want to talk in peace?

JULIE

I want you to give it up. It won't be the same . . .

She turns away to hide her tears. Olivier hands her a handkerchief. Julie helplessly accepts it and wipes her eyes.

OLIVIER

I'll tell you why I agreed to try. Because I only agreed to try. I
don't know if I'll finish. It was the only way . . . I thought . . .
it was a way to make you want something. Or not want it.
Anything. To make you run. Make you cry, run after my car.

*Julie pulls the handkerchief away from her eyes, looks at Olivier
angrily.*

JULIE

That's not fair.

OLIVIER

No, it's not. But you didn't leave me any choice.

Julie nods slowly several times; it is true.

Do you want to see what I've done? I've started writing.

JULIE

Yes.

INT. OLIVIER'S FLAT. DAY

*Olivier is playing the piano. Julie stands leaning against the instrument
with her eyes shut. Her finger touches the coloured copy of the score
which she had once destroyed. The marks made by the blue felt-tip pen
are the same as on the original – bright, clearly visible. What Olivier
plays are twenty to thirty seconds of good music. He finishes and looks
questioningly at Julie. She opens her eyes, it is difficult to say whether
she was concentrating only on the music.*

JULIE

Did you read it carefully?

She points to the copy of Patrick's score lying on the piano.

OLIVIER

Dozens of times.

JULIE

I'll tell you the idea behind it. It's the sheer scale,
unparalleled as yet. You're standing on the Etoile. There are
a thousand members of an orchestra, choirs and eleven

76

enormous television screens the size of a five-storeyed
building in front of you. There are a thousand musicians on
every one of these: in Berlin, London, Brussels, Rome or
Madrid . . .

OLIVIER

I know. Patrick told me several times.

JULIE

You know . . . For a concert like that to work the music has
to rise several inches off the ground. Or even higher. Imagine:
twelve thousand musicians waiting for a sign from you.
Crowds everywhere. You lower the baton and everywhere the
music starts all at once . . .

OLIVIER

A choir in Athens.

JULIE

Yes . . .

OLIVIER

Do you know what the chorus was supposed to sing?

*Julie smiles, surprised that Olivier doesn't know. She looks around the
room and goes up to the extensive library.*

JULIE

I thought he told you everything.

*She finds a dark bound book on the bottom shelf. She flicks through for
a moment, finds the right page and lays it in front of Olivier.*

In Greek, the rhythm's a bit different, of course.

*Olivier, reading a few lines from the book, quietly plays on the piano.
He brightens up. He repeats the music a few times, muttering the
incomprehensible words and, impressed by the discovery, lifts his eyes up
to Julie. Julie looks at him with the expression of someone who does not
see what she is looking at.*

OLIVIER

Julie . . .

Julie comes to.

JULIE

Who was that girl?

OLIVIER

Who?

JULIE

The girl in the photographs on the programme. She was with
Patrick.

*Olivier turns, surprised by the question. Julie moves from where she was
standing, walks round the piano and leans over straight in front of
Olivier.*

I'll find out. It won't be hard.

OLIVIER

Didn't you know?

JULIE

No.

*Olivier gets up from the piano, takes a few steps, stands in front of the
window.*

OLIVIER

Everyone knew . . .

Julie goes up to him.

JULIE

Just tell me. Were they together?

OLIVIER

Yes.

JULIE

Since when?

OLIVIER

A few years.

What Julie suspected when the photographs of Patrick with the fair-haired girl flashed across the TV for a few seconds is confirmed.

JULIE

Who is she? Where does she live?

Olivier remains silent for a moment, but knows he cannot avoid answering.

OLIVIER

Somewhere in Montparnasse. They often met at the courts. She's a lawyer, or works for one. What do you want to do?

Julie smiles, she wants the smile to be natural but somehow does not manage it.

JULIE

Meet her.

EXT. IN FRONT OF THE PALACE OF JUSTICE. DAY

Julie runs up the wide steps of the Palace of Justice. She stops at the top and looks down. It is quite busy. She looks carefully and methodically at the faces of people going up and going down. She moves her position in order to see better. Obviously giving up, she goes inside.

INT. PALACE OF JUSTICE. DAY

Just as she did on the steps, Julie studies those around her as she crosses the huge hall of the Palace. It is the first time she has been here. She catches sight of an arrow pointing towards the bar and goes in that direction.

Julie crosses the bar. Quite unceremoniously she looks at the faces of people sitting at the tables. She approaches the Barmaid.

JULIE

A packet of Marlboro, please.

The Barmaid disappears into the back. Julie studies the customers' faces again. She takes the cigarettes from the Barmaid and, without looking, hands her the change.

Julie lights a cigarette at the crossing of two wide corridors with dozens of doors leading to courtrooms. It is a good observation point. She now inhales with obvious know-how and pleasure. Using the ashtray there as a pretext, she watches both corridors. For a moment, her attention is drawn by a young man in slightly too long trousers who is moving along the corridor nervously. He is obviously lost and for a moment makes Julie laugh. It is Karol – the main character from Three Colours: White. *He runs off down the corridor. After a while, at the end of the small corridor, Julie catches a brief glimpse of a young, fair-haired woman. She immediately goes in that direction. She turns the corner and sees Sandrine on a bench by the window. She is in the company of an elderly, solemn lawyer in a gown. They are talking to a young woman, obviously their client. It is Dominique, one of the characters in* Three Colours: White. *Sandrine is sitting with her back to Julie and although Julie does not see her clearly, she is sure she is the woman she is looking for. The entire group gets up and disappears through the door of a courtroom near by. Julie waits for a moment then approaches the door. There on the cause list she finds the names of the parties and lawyers. Among them she finds Sandrine's name. Julie quietly opens the door and goes in.*

INT. COURTROOM. DAY

Julie sits on a back bench watching Sandrine. Karol is testifying in front of the court. Obviously nervous, he raises his voice.

KAROL
(in Polish)
Where's the equality? Is it because I can't speak French that
the court won't listen to my case?

*In a monotonous voice, a Translator translates this into French. The
Judge studies Karol carefully. We, however, only see this trial
fragmentarily, from Julie's point of view. We mainly observe Sandrine
who, taking notes, exchanges short comments with her patron. Julie
leaves the room.*

*(Note: The scenes from the Palace of Justice are described in detail. This
is due to the necessity of describing characters and situations important
for* Three Colours: White *– in the film the scenes will be short, concise
and rhythmic.)*

EXT. PARIS STREET. DAY

*Julie follows Sandrine, her patron and two other acquaintances.
Keeping a distance of a dozen steps or more, Julie notices that
Sandrine's gait is somewhat heavy. The entire group disappears in the
door of a restaurant near the courts. Julie follows them.*

INT. RESTAURANT. DAY

*The restaurant is crowded at this time of day. Julie finds a place a few
tables away from Sandrine, sits down and lights another cigarette.
Sandrine laughs loudly at some joke which the elderly lawyer has
made. Julie grimaces a little. Still laughing, Sandrine squeezes by and
goes to the washroom. Julie, without thinking twice, gets up and
follows her.*

INT. RESTAURANT WASHROOM. DAY

*Julie waits by one of the mirrors in the spacious washroom with a
cigarette in her mouth. Sandrine emerges from one of the cubicles and it
is only now that Julie realizes that Sandrine is in the last weeks of
pregnancy. Sandrine rinses her hands under the tap, shakes them out
instead of drying them under the drier and opens the door.*

JULIE
Excuse me.

Sandrine stops, surprised.

> SANDRINE
>
> Yes?

Julie shakes her finger, looking Sandrine straight in the eyes and Sandrine, still surprised, takes a few steps towards her.

> Yes . . .

> JULIE
>
> You were my husband's mistress?

Sandrine looks at her carefully, recognizes her. She smiles.

> SANDRINE
>
> Yes.

She says this so naturally that the tension between them disappears.

> JULIE
>
> I didn't know. I just found out that . . .

> SANDRINE
>
> It's a shame. Now you'll hate him, and me, too.

> JULIE
>
> I don't know . . .

> SANDRINE
>
> Yes, you will.

Julie looks down at Sandrine's swollen belly. Sandrine, sensing her eyes, puts her hand over her belly.

> JULIE
>
> Is it his . . .?

> SANDRINE
>
> Yes. But he didn't know. I only found out after the accident . . . I didn't want a child, but it's happened. Now I want to keep it.

At that moment, a middle-aged woman walks into the washroom. Julie and Sandrine fall silent; they do not move. They hear muffled noises from the cubicle. Sandrine smiles knowingly at Julie, who cannot help but smile too. The woman flushes the chain, emerges from the cubicle and, smiling, rinses her hands. For a while longer she makes a noise with the hand-drier and leaves.

Do you have a cigarette?

Julie takes out her packet and offers one to Sandrine. She nods at her belly.

JULIE

Isn't it bad for . . .?

Sandrine smiles gently and lights her cigarette.

SANDRINE

Do you want to know when and where he slept with me? How often?

JULIE

No . . .

SANDRINE

You want to know if he loved me?

JULIE

Yes. That's what I wanted to ask you. But now I don't have to. I know he did.

SANDRINE

Yes. He did.

Julie makes her way towards the door. Sandrine stops her.

Julie . . .

Julie looks at her.

Will you hate me now?

Julie makes a vague movement with her head and, leaving the washroom, loudly closes the door.

INT./EXT. METRO STATION. DAY

A ticket is inserted and spewed out by the machine. Julie's hand takes the ticket.

*A low-level camera photographs the crowd on the platform for a second.
With a tremendous din, an underground train speeds towards the
camera and 'runs over' it, the carriages roll by. The train stops, after a
while it moves off.*

*The carriage is crowded. We scan a number of faces before we reach
Julie, standing, squashed in the crowd. The train emerges from
underground. An unnaturally bright, busy town. Julie's face equally
bright.*

EXT./INT. REST-HOME. DUSK

*Julie passes through the gate of the rest-home which we already know.
She passes the building, approaches the window from the park side. She
presses her face against the glass. Inside, her Mother, in a comfortable
armchair, is staring attentively at the TV. Julie glances at the
programme which her Mother is watching. She sees the acute slant of
the screen, which stands straight in front of her Mother. On TV we see
the well-known cityscape of Manhattan. Only after a while does Julie
realize what the subject of the programme is. A rope is attached to the
tops of two skyscrapers. Dozens of storeys above the street, a man steps
on to the rope and, balancing himself, moves forward one step at a time.
Julie's Mother, tense, leans towards the TV. Julie, her eyes glazed over
with tears, watches her a moment longer then moves away from the
window. She passes the gate and disappears into the tree-lined avenue,
dark at this time of day.*

INT. OLIVIER'S FLAT. NIGHT

*Dark. The front door bell. The bell rings again – for a long time; the
door opens. In the bright rectangle of light we see Julie in Olivier's
doorway.*

OLIVIER
Come in. Please . . .

Julie does not move from the door.

Has anything happened?

Julie shakes her head, but does not move.

84

You met her?

JULIE

Yes.

Olivier waits, thinking that Julie will want to tell him about the meeting. Julie is waiting, no doubt, for some sort of reaction from Olivier as to what she has found out, but he has known for a long time. Nothing happens.

Have you made any headway? With the music.

OLIVIER

Yes.

JULIE

Will you show me?

OLIVIER

I will . . .

Julie enters, throws off her jacket and goes straight to the piano where scores, writing materials, coffee, cigarettes are spread out. Olivier makes a gesture as if to offer her something to drink, but Julie shakes her head.

JULIE

Once . . . You asked me to take Patrick's papers.

OLIVIER

You didn't want to.

JULIE

No, I didn't. If I had . . . Were the photographs among them?

Olivier nods.

If I'd taken them, I'd have known then. If I'd burnt them without looking, I'd never have known.

OLIVIER

That's right.

Julie smiles unexpectedly, lights a cigarette.

JULIE

Maybe it's better this way. Will you play it for me? The bit you composed?

Olivier sits at the piano and plays the first few notes. Julie leans forward to see the score on the stand. Olivier passes the score to her.

OLIVIER

I remember it all.

JULIE

Right. You always remembered everything.

Julie looks at the lines of the score, densely filled in in tiers. We hear several bars of the introduction and Julie's question.

(*off*)

Are those the basses?

OLIVIER
(*off*)

The altos.

JULIE
(*off*)

Again please? From the beginning . . .

*Olivier (on soundtrack) stops and we see Julie's finger returning to the
beginning of the line. We hear the sound of altos and Julie's hand moves
along the staves with the developing music. This lasts – let us say –
seven seconds.*

OLIVIER
(*off*)

And now . . .

*At this moment Julie's finger comes up to the place where notes start on
all the staves of the score. The entire orchestra resounds with tremendous
impact (on soundtrack). It sound good and strong – especially as we
continue to watch details of the score on screen. We listen to a dozen or
so seconds of music in this way. At a certain moment, of course – when
the audience has understood the principle by which the music is being
introduced – we leave the details of the score and also see Julie and
Olivier.*

JULIE
(*interrupting*)
Wait a moment . . .

As soon as Olivier lifts his fingers from the keyboard the entire huge orchestra immediately falls silent.

What if we tried it a bit lighter? Without the percussion . . .

Olivier hits the keyboard and the orchestra (on soundtrack) takes off – but this time it sounds simpler, clearer. We do not hear the previously booming brass. They both listen closely.

And without trumpets?

The trumpets disappear from the music (on soundtrack).

No. Leave one.

One trumpet resounds in the orchestra.

Violins a bit quieter. Sul-poticello . . .

We hear the violins play much more sharply.

Or sul-tasto.

Now the violins sound wonderful. The music is much nobler, purer. Julie listens, gently moving her hand as if she were conducting.

Let's change the piano.

OLIVIER
For what?

Julie thinks, listening.

JULIE
A flute. From the letter 'A'.

The music falls silent, Julie's finger moves back a few bars and moves forward again, this time with a flute as leading instrument. It sounds like the one that they had once listened to together in the café. The Flautist played like this. Now, together with the orchestra, he sounds disquieting, yet beautiful.

And now . . . A pause.

The music falls silent.

Ah . . . can you hear it? Silence.

At a signal from Julie, the orchestra starts again, playing another dozen or so seconds before Olivier breaks off.

OLIVIER

That's as far as I got.

JULIE

And the finale?

OLIVIER

I don't know.

JULIE

There was a slip of paper . . .

Olivier looks through the scores with blue marks on it, which lay on the side all this time. Of course, there's no slip of paper there. Julie realizes that it cannot be there. The Copyist did not get hold of it, so she could not have copied it. She interrupts Olivier's search.

It's not there. I've got it. I forgot.

She takes it out of her handbag and straightens out the slip of music folded in four.

It was a counterpoint that was supposed to come back at the finale.

Olivier reads the notes. Smiles.

OLIVIER

Van den Budenmayer?

JULIE

You know how much he loved him. Not just because of his music, but because of his tragic life and his premonition of misery. He wanted to remind people of him at the end of the concert. He said it's a memento. Try weaving it back in.

Olivier raises his eyes. He holds the slip of paper out to her. Julie smiles and shakes her head. The paper remains in Olivier's hand.

OLIVIER

Thanks.

Julie turns serious.

JULIE

Are you still in touch with our lawyer?

OLIVIER

From time to time . . .

JULIE

Do you know whether he's sold the house yet?

OLIVIER

I don't know. I doubt it. He'd have called me.

JULIE

Ask him to hold on.

OLIVIER

Okay . . .

He looks at her, intrigued. Julie waves her hand.

JULIE

It's not important. If you can handle all this . . .

She indicates Patrick's and Olivier's scores and the slip of music which Olivier is still holding in his hand.

Will you show me?

OLIVIER

Of course, I'll show you.

JULIE

I'd like to look at it in peace. At home. You know where I live. Top floor.

OLIVIER

I'll bring it over.

EXT. JULIE'S HOUSE. DAY

Julie in front of her house. She has not been here for a long time. She

*scans the house, obviously waiting for somebody. The Gardener opens
the blinds on the ground floor. In front of the open gate a small car stops
uncertainly. Someone inside checks the house number or notices Julie
because the car turns and slowly drives through the gate and stops near
her. Sandrine climbs out. They greet each other.*

JULIE

Have you been here before?

SANDRINE

Never.

*Julie nods, that is what she thought. The Gardener is now opening the
blinds on the first floor, the windows gleam one by one.*

SANDRINE

I didn't think you'd want to see me again . . .

JULIE

But I did. I want to show you something.

*They make their way towards the house. On the steps they pass the
Gardener who is just coming out.*

GARDENER

There was a mattress here . . .

JULIE

Yes.

GARDENER

It's gone. Olivier came and bought it. I didn't think you'd
need it any more.

Julie receives this information with a smile.

JULIE

That's fine.

INT. JULIE'S HOUSE. DAY

*Julie shows Sandrine around an entirely empty house. She shows her the
various rooms, halls, quarters.*

JULIE

This is the living-room. This the kitchen and larder.
Bathroom. Stairs to the first floor. There are three bedrooms
up there, and a study. Upstairs on the garden side are the
guest rooms.

*Sandrine does not understand Julie's intentions at all. She looks at
everything that Julie shows her with increasing amazement. They stop
at a first-floor window, look down – a beautiful view. Masses of
greenery, the city somewhere in the distance. Julie asks quietly.*

Is it a boy or a girl? Do you know?

SANDRINE

A boy.

JULIE

Have you chosen a name?

SANDRINE

Yes.

They remain silent for a while. Sandrine does not feel comfortable in the situation. She looks at Julie suspiciously.

JULIE

I thought he ought to have his name. And his house. Here.

Julie indicates with her hand what she has in mind. Sandrine smiles, looking at Julie. Julie does not understand the smile. She looks at her, surprised. Sandrine starts laughing.

SANDRINE

I knew it.

JULIE

What?

SANDRINE

Patrick told me a lot about you . . .

JULIE

What?

SANDRINE

That you're good . . . That you're so good and kind-hearted . . . And that that's what you want to be. People can always count on you. Even me . . .

She notices that Julie is looking at her coldly. Sandrine makes as if to hug her but stops short. She doesn't take her eyes off Julie.

I'm sorry.

INT. JULIE'S FLAT. NIGHT

Julie's face. She is intent and at the same time a little excited. Leaning over a large table, she lifts her head and closes her eyes, bites her lips as if she were trying to imagine or grasp something. Her lips tremble. This lasts a while, then she leans over the table again. We look over her shoulder. On the table a dozen or so pages of the score lie spread out. Julie has a thick felt-tip pen in her hand. Carefully, one step at a time, she makes her blue marks. At times she crosses out entire passages of too rich instrumentation, at times adds notes, at times changes the instruments or scale in which they will one day play. All this takes place in total silence. We hear only the rustle of paper and the sharp, irritating

93

squeak of the felt-tip. Julie reaches the end of the score. The music now looks like Patrick's music which we have already seen several times in the film – perhaps there are even more blue marks, lines and words than there were on the other scores. Julie reaches for the telephone and this time punches out the number from memory, automatically. We hear Olivier's voice.

JULIE

It's me. I've finished. You can pick it up tomorrow morning. Or today, if you're not too tired.

INTERCUT WITH OLIVIER'S FLAT. NIGHT

OLIVIER

I'm not tired. But I won't pick the score up.

JULIE
(*off*)

What?

OLIVIER

I won't pick it up. I've been thinking about it all week. This music can be mine. A bit too heavy and awkward perhaps, but mine. Or yours, but we've got to make it clear.

Julie remains silent, stunned by this piece of news.

OLIVIER

Are you there?

INT. JULIE'S FLAT. NIGHT

JULIE

Yes. You're right.

Julie puts the phone down without saying goodbye. She gets up from the table quite abruptly and moves across the room. She goes back, takes a packet of Marlboro from her bag, lights a cigarette and immediately, barely having lit it, stubs it out in the ashtray. She goes to the kitchen, searches for something on the shelf and finds a flower vase. She fills it with water and stands it on the table. Some blue flowers, still wrapped in Cellophane, lie in the hall. Julie unwraps the Cellophane and puts the flowers in the water. She smiles faintly at

94

what she has just done and reaches for the phone again. She redials the number she had punched out a moment ago. Olivier answers. Julie speaks without preliminaries, but also without the previous sternness or hardness.

> JULIE
>
> Olivier, it's me again. I wanted to ask you . . . Is it true that you're sleeping on the mattress . . .?

> OLIVIER
> (*off*)
>
> Yes.

> JULIE
>
> You never told me.

> OLIVIER
> (*off*)
>
> No . . .

> JULIE
>
> Do you still love me?

> OLIVIER
> (*off*)
>
> I do.

> JULIE
>
> Are you alone?

> OLIVIER
> (*off*)
>
> Of course I'm alone.

> JULIE
>
> I'm coming over.

She replaces the receiver. She puts on her coat and scarf, goes up to the table and gathers the score lying there. She touches the first note with her finger. At that moment we hear the music. It is that part of the concert composed by Patrick. Julie leads us with her finger to the place where the first words of the choir appear.

CHORUS
(*off; in Greek*)

Though I speak with
the tongues of men and of angels,
and have not charity,
I am become as sounding brass,
or a tinkling cymbal.
(*New Testament*, 1st Letter to the Corinthians, 13)

Gathering the music under her arm, Julie switches off the light. It becomes completely dark.

INT. OLIVIER'S FLAT. DAWN

It is still dark. We hear the next verse.

CHORUS
(*off*)

And though I have the
gift of prophecy,
and understand all mysteries,
and all knowledge;
and though I have all faith
so that I could remove mountains,
and have not charity,
I am nothing.

Very slowly it grows lighter; we begin to sense the first signs of dawn.

Charity suffereth long,
and is kind; charity envieth not;
charity vaunteth not itself, is not
puffed up,
Beareth all things, believeth all
things, hopeth all things, endureth
all things.
Charity never faileth;
but whether there be prophecies, they
shall fail;
whether there be tongues, they shall
cease;

whether there be knowledge, it shall
vanish away.
And now abideth faith, hope, charity,
these three;
but the greatest of these is charity.

*We recognize – or rather sense where we are – in Olivier's flat. The
score, thrown around negligently, lies on the piano, on the floor. We
distinguish the shapes of furniture and objects. The music – now without
the choir – is magnificent and beautiful. We experience what Julie was
saying – it rises several inches off the ground. The camera slowly moves
across the still dark objects of the flat. It discovers Julie and Olivier in
bed. Their bodies and faces are barely visible in the light of the breaking
day. Julie opens her eyes and, as at the beginning of the film, watches
Olivier. After a little while, she realizes where she is and what must
have happened that night. She frowns a little. The camera again tracks
slowly . . . gets darker.*

MIX TO:

INT. ANTOINE'S FLAT. DAWN

*From the mix, the camera continues to track from the previous scene.
The music continues. We hear the sharp ringing of an alarm clock. The
camera reaches Antoine who is getting up at dawn. Still half
unconscious, he sits on his bed. From his neck hangs the gold cross which
Julie gave him. He touches the cross and sits as if engrossed in the
music. The camera slowly moves, leaves Antoine.*

MIX TO:

INT. REST-HOME. DAY

*From the mix, the camera tracks to Julie's Mother sitting in her
armchair, no doubt watching TV. Continuation of the music. Julie's
Mother closes her eyes and doesn't open them any more, although we
stay with her for quite a long time. The camera tracks.*

MIX TO:

INT. CABARET LIVE-SHOW. NIGHT

From the mix, the camera tracks to Lucille, who is waiting for her entry on stage. She has turned her head. We move around her and find her looking somewhere ahead, into the distance. Continuation of the music. The camera tracks, we leave Lucille.

    MIX TO:

INT. SANDRINE'S FLAT. NIGHT

From the mix, the camera slowly tracks to the naked belly of a woman in the last phases of pregnancy. Sandrine's hand touches her belly, wanting to feel the baby move. From the belly, across a book, we track to Sandrine's face. She smiles. We pass her face.

    MIX TO:

INT. OLIVIER'S FLAT. DAWN

From the mix, it's dawn again. Again we track across what we discern to be furniture in Olivier's flat. We come to the bed. Olivier is peacefully asleep. He is alone. He moves a little in his sleep. We leave him, the camera tracks slowly, as it does throughout the sequence. Furniture, floor, we track in a definite direction. In the music, the theme which Julie called the memento resounds. The rhythm is slower and from the music of the joyous hymn about love which – according to Patrick – could be the salvation of Europe and of the world, it becomes serious, announces something dark, dangerous. By the window, we find Julie, her face in her hands. One by one, tears appear on these hands. Julie is crying helplessly.

    FADE OUT.

    END CREDITS on the last passage of music.

Three Colours: White

CREDITS

CAST

KAROL	Zbigniew Zamachowski
DOMINIQUE	Julie Delpy
JUREK	Jerzy Stuhr

CREW

Director	Krzysztof Kieślowski
Screenplay	Krzysztof Kieślowski, Krzysztof Piesiewicz
Cinematography	Edward Kłosiński
Editor	Urszula Lesiak
Art Director	Claude Lenoir
Music	Zbigniew Preisner
Sound	Jean-Claude Laureaux
Sound Mixer	William Flageollet
Executive Producer	Yvon Crenn
Producer	Marin Karmitz
Production Companies	Tor Productions/MK2 Productions SA/CED Productions/France 3 Cinema/CAB Productions

EXT. PARIS STREET. DAY

A wild crowd outside the department stores in the city centre. A terrible noise, vendors shouting, street organs grinding, children crying. Hell. The camera observes this sea of faces slightly from above. Slowly it distinguishes Karol from among the crowd. He approaches closer, cranes his neck and, using the camera as a mirror, scrutinizes himself. He is not tall, his trousers are a little too long and his jacket is not well pressed. He appraises himself critically. Deciding to improve this state of affairs, he makes his way towards the entrance of the department store. Again we see masses of people throng by.

Against this background: TITLE CREDITS.

The camera slowly tracks downwards. Karol leaves the department store with a small carrier bag in his hand. He pulls out a tie, approaches closer. Again using the camera as a mirror, he attempts to tie the tie. The result is a clumsy, lumpish knot. Karol tears the tie off his neck and renews his efforts. This time the result is better. Karol takes out a comb and arranges his hair, combs it confidently, with pleasure. He does not need the little, round mirror with the usual photograph of a starlet on the back, which he carries in the same pocket as his comb. Happy with the result, he pulls a face at himself: everything is going to be fine.

EXT. IN FRONT OF THE PALACE OF JUSTICE. DAY

Karol hesitates for a moment in front of the formidable stairs and the mighty building of the Palace of Justice. He makes his way up, trying not to frighten the pigeons on the stairs. One of the pigeons takes off with a flutter of wings. Karol watches its flight with the hint of a smile, brightens up as the pigeon flies over him, then suddenly grows serious. With a slight splutter, a white stain appears on his shoulder. Karol wipes it off with a clean handkerchief. Uncertain of the effect, he disappears through the enormous Palace doors.

INT. PALACE OF JUSTICE. DAY

Karol winds his way through the corridors. He scrutinizes the notices on the cause lists, studies each one for a moment, obviously lost. Glancing at his watch, he speeds up his search. He passes Julie (the main character from Three Colours: Blue) *– he does not know her, so he does not particularly notice her among the other people in the corridor. Around one of the corners, he comes across Dominique sitting by a window. She is talking to a respectable lawyer in a gown and his apprentice, Sandrine. Dominique catches sight of Karol. Karol tries to smile, points questioningly in the direction of the courtroom. Dominique solemnly nods, yes, it is here. Karol looks at her anxiously for a while; Dominique smiles derisively, making a strange gesture near her hair – as if pretending to cut it. Karol then suddenly pulls a face and doubles up. He dashes to the toilet, passing Julie who is approaching down the corridor.*

INT. TOILET. DAY

Bent over the toilet bowl, Karol is throwing up. His stomach is turning inside out. He is kneeling, his head resting against the cistern. He is pale, breathing heavily. He flushes the toilet.

He drinks some water from the tap, cleans his teeth with his fingers. Glancing at the mirror, he once more arranges his hair using his comb and gathers himself together. There is no way out, he has got to prove himself equal to the task ahead.

INT. COURTROOM. DAY

The trial is in progress. There are several people in the large, impressive room. Karol looks all the more miserable here. The Judge is obviously tired and a little impatient. He interrupts Dominique, who is testifying.

JUDGE
Can you please give us concrete reasons for wanting a divorce?

DOMINIQUE
Concrete?

JUDGE
Yes. Concrete.

Dominique glances at Karol and sighs. She lowers her eyes, hesitates a moment and, looking at the Judge, says.

DOMINIQUE
Our marriage hasn't been consummated.

The Judge winces; this case won't be easy. Karol does not take his eyes off Dominique.

FLASHBACK – INT. HALL OF A HAIRDRESSING CONTEST. NIGHT

Through flashing scissors, combs, hairdryers, we see Dominique's face among those of the other girls whose hair is being styled at a hairdressing contest. It is obviously a subjective point of view. Feeling Karol's (the camera's) eyes on her, Dominique turns. Looking straight at the camera, she smiles, tilting her head a little.

INT. COURTROOM. DAY

The Judge's voice wakes Karol from his daydream.

JUDGE
Your name and surname?

Karol rises. The Interpreter, without troubling himself too much, translates the question.

KAROL
Karol Karol.

JUDGE
I beg your pardon?

KAROL
My name and surname are the same.

The Judge looks at his papers, and nods; that is correct.

JUDGE
So be it. Nationality?

KAROL

I gave up my Polish nationality and am trying . . . I'm in the process of trying to get a French one.

The Interpreter translates without moving from his place. The procedure with the Interpreter continues throughout the whole scene in court.

JUDGE

Your profession?

KAROL

I'm a master hairdresser. I've got international recognition . . . I've won competitions . . .

Karol pulls some papers out of his pocket, no doubt wanting to prove these accomplishments, but the Judge stops him midway. ˊ

JUDGE

Is your wife's testimony true to the facts?

Karol fills his lungs with air and lets it out. He puts the papers away again. He looks at Dominique, who is sitting with her eyes lowered. Karol turns away.

KAROL

In a manner of speaking. But before, in Poland, when we met
and here at the beginning, too . . . I think I satisfied my wife.
It's only later that . . .

JUDGE

I want to establish the facts. Is what your wife said true? Has
your marriage been consummated?

Karol looks at Dominique, who also looks into his eyes.

KAROL

No.

JUDGE

When did intercourse stop?

KAROL

Intercourse . . . We haven't made love since we got married.
That is . . . I stopped being able to. It's just temporary.

JUDGE

When was the marriage contracted?

Karol does not take his eyes off Dominique.

KAROL

Half a year ago.

FLASHBACK – INT. AIRPORT. DAY

*Dominique's face glued to a glass pane at the airport. Looking straight
into the camera she recognizes Karol. Laughing, radiant, she points to
where they are to meet. The camera tracks in the direction shown by
Dominique and, among other people, catches sight of Dominique
running with her arms thrown open in greeting. Dominique runs into the
camera, nimbly overtaking all the other waiting people. At that moment
the camera backs away a little. We see Dominique snuggle up to Karol,
and Karol embrace her, dropping the bags and suitcases he has been
carrying.*

INT. COURTROOM. DAY

Karol is distracted for a moment by the sound of the door opening at the back of the room. Julie enters and sits in the back row of pews. Karol picks up his interrupted train of thought.

KAROL

I'd like to explain. One of the reasons could be my work. I'm working twelve hours a day here, sometimes longer. It's unheard of in Poland. Maybe it's a matter of being over-worked. A few days' rest . . .

The Judge nods, agreeing with this diagnosis and again signals for Karol to sit down. No doubt he is irritated by the fact that every one of Karol's words has to be translated. Karol obediently sits down, but immediately raises his finger, indicating that he wants to continue speaking. The Judge thumps his fist on the table but Karol, instead of being silenced, jumps up. He speaks louder than before.

Where's the equality? Is it because I can't speak French that the court won't listen to my case?

The Judge, having listened to the translation of this protest, scrutinizes Karol carefully.

JUDGE

What is it that you want?

KAROL

I want to have my say. I want to be given a chance.

JUDGE

Concerning the case?

KAROL

Yes.

The Judge, without enthusiasm, expresses his agreement with a nod. Julie quietly leaves the room.

I need time, Your Honour. I want to save our marriage. I don't believe our feelings for each other have disappeared. But I need time. One night I was ready to . . .

He is moved by what he is saying or perhaps by the memories of that evening. His voice trembles. The Judge notices his state and does not interrupt him. He waits. Karol is in no condition to continue. The Judge asks gently.

JUDGE

Was the marriage consummated that night?

KAROL

No.

JUDGE

So what's this got to do with the case?

KAROL

Nothing.

JUDGE

Unfortunately, nothing. You started to talk about feelings. The court understands the state of your feelings. And you, Madame?

Dominique did not expect any more questions. She gets up, disorientated.

DOMINIQUE

I beg your pardon?

JUDGE

Do you love your husband?

Dominique does not answer for a moment. Then she speaks quietly.

DOMINIQUE

I used to . . .

Karol watches her with even greater anxiety than before.

JUDGE

And now?

DOMINIQUE

No. Not any more.

Karol sits down, rests his head on his hands and talks to himself, quietly.

KAROL

Oh God . . .

FLASHBACK – INT./EXT. CHURCH. DAY

The dark interior of a church with the tiny, bright point of the door in the middle. The camera (from Karol's point of view) tracks towards this bright point which grows larger with every step. From time to time the veil of Dominique's wedding dress appears ahead of it for a moment. The camera reaches the door, tracks into the light. Handfuls of rice rain down on it. From the right-hand side, Dominique's face appears. It comes closer to kiss Karol and obscures the picture.

INT. COURTROOM. DAY

Karol, still holding his head in his hands, makes a tiny gap between his fingers. In this way he can see Dominique get up from the bench. Dominique uncrosses her legs, stocking suspenders flash, and a bit of thigh. Karol closes his eyes and presses his hands into his face.

WHITE

EXT. IN FRONT OF THE PALACE OF JUSTICE. DAY

*Karol, blinded by the sun, descends the long steps of the Palace of
Justice. Irritated, wretched, he trips on one of the steps and barely
regains his balance. From halfway down the steps he notices a car
waiting below, copious fumes emanating from its exhaust. Karol stops a
moment, automatically wanting to escape, then walks down. The car is
a white Polonez (a Polish middle-class car) with Warsaw number-
plates. Dominique climbs out and pulls out an enormous, not very heavy
suitcase from the boot. She stands it next to the car and gets back inside
when Karol is already close by.*

DOMINIQUE

That's all.

*Karol, looking at Dominique all the while, takes a few steps in her
direction, but Dominique merely waves her fingers goodbye and leaves.
It is only now that Karol realizes the finality of the separation. He grabs
his enormous case and runs after the departing Polonez.*

KAROL
(*shouting*)

Dominique! Dominique!

*The Polonez drives away. Karol runs a while longer and then tired,
seeing the futility of the chase, squats down and leans his head against
the suitcase so as to hide his tears. He gets up. With the enormous
suitcase, he walks into the street. He does not know whether to go right
or left, so he goes straight ahead, paying no attention to the hooting cars
which just about manage to miss him.*

EXT. IN FRONT OF THE BANK. DUSK

*It gets dark early at this time of year. Karol, with his baggage, stops in
front of a grand bank on a relatively quiet street. He looks just as
insignificant here as he did in the enormous courtroom. Not far from the
doors of the bank is a cashpoint machine. Karol stands his suitcase on
the pavement and finds his credit card hidden deep in the lining of his
jacket. From the back pocket of his trousers he takes out a used metro
ticket where he has noted his secret PIN number. He mutters the four
numbers to himself several times. With reverence, careful not to make a
mistake, he slips the card into the cashpoint machine. He then gently*

presses his finger on the PIN numbers and waits with outspread fingers. The machine grinds away for a moment, words incomprehensible to Karol appear on the screen and suddenly a metal lid majestically closes the machine without dispensing either money or card. At the last minute, Karol, horrified, tries to salvage whatever he can; he blindly presses the keys but the lid nearly clamps his fingers. Karol tears his hand out and thumps his fist against the machine. In vain. A Clerk appears in the door. Karol calms down, indicates that the machine has swallowed his card. The Clerk smiles.

CLERK

Come inside, please.

Karol makes a move, taking his baggage with him.

INT. BANK. DUSK

All the workings of the cashpoint machine are inside the bank. The Clerk opens the lid and finds Karol's credit card. He reads the name printed on the card.

CLERK

Karol Karol?

Karol eagerly nods his head. But the Clerk does not return the card.

Your account has been blocked.

Concentrating in order to understand what is being said to him in French, Karol has no doubts as to one point. He repeats in disbelief.

KAROL

Blocked . . .

CLERK

Yes. Blocked. Your card's invalid.

The Clerk, seeing that Karol does not speak French all that well, draws an 'X' in the air – invalid, cancelled. Karol holds his hand out for the card.

KAROL

My card. My money.

The Clerk repeats the 'X' sign and with a pair of large scissors cuts the invalid card into little pieces. Hearing the unpleasant sound of plastic being cut, Karol shudders as shivers go down his back. The Clerk throws the cut-up card into the bin. With a smile, he watches Karol, who does not move, but is transfixed.

CLERK
Courage!

EXT. IN FRONT OF THE BANK. NIGHT

Karol sits, motionless, on his suitcase in front of the closed bank. On the other side of the street he notices a well-dressed Old Man who, with a large bottle in his hand, approaches a green receptacle for glass. He gets up on tiptoes and tries to put the bottle into the rubber opening. He is a bit too old and a bit too hunchbacked to reach. He jumps up clumsily, in vain. His efforts obviously improve Karol's frame of mind. He smiles unpleasantly. The bottle stays stuck halfway in the opening, the Old Man walks away. Karol, revitalized, checks out his possessions. In his pockets he finds several coins. He is intrigued – after taking his hand out with the coins, something is still clinking in his pocket. He reaches deeper, his arm goes down almost to the elbow. He pulls out two small keys, linked together with a colourful, plastic ring. A surprise. Karol brightens up.

EXT. IN FRONT OF DOMINIQUE'S HAIRDRESSING SALON. DAY

A busy, relatively smart street. The white Polonez parks skilfully in the little free space. Dominique climbs out, takes out some keys from her handbag and approaches the lowered metal shutters. She notices with surprise that the padlock is not in its usual place. She raises the shutters effortlessly. With the second key she unlocks the door and enters.

INT. DOMINIQUE'S HAIRDRESSING SALON. DAY

She automatically pulls open the blinds, turns around and freezes. Karol has pulled two hairdressing chairs together and is lying asleep, covered with an overall. He wakes up, blinded for a moment by the bright light; stretches and sees Dominique. He smiles. Dominique does not move. Karol lifts his hand with the keys on a plastic ring and clinks them provocatively. Dominique picks up the telephone receiver.

KAROL

No.

He holds out his hand with the keys to Dominique. She replaces the receiver and slowly approaches Karol. She wants to take the keys and at that moment Karol grabs her hand and pulls her to him. Dominique resists, Karol tugs. With his other hand he pushes the overalls aside and finally manages to place Dominique's hand on his flies. Dominique stiffens. Karol releases his grip, finally lets her hand go altogether. For a moment Dominique does not move; she looks at Karol surprised and slowly starts to stroke the place where her hand is. Under the influence of the caress, Karol closes his eyes. Dominique fiddles with his flies – we feel her movements rather than actually see them – slips off her shoes, removes her knickers and short skirt and, wearing only her long blouse which covers the essential parts, she sits on Karol. She lowers her head over him. Karol touches her hair and – judging by Dominique's reaction, this is what their foreplay consisted of before – skilfully plaits two braids. Dominique is getting more and more excited. Karol touches her ears, her nose and her mouth with the tips of the braids. They both begin to breathe more and more heavily. Dominique unbuttons her blouse, freeing her breasts, lifts herself a little and suddenly freezes. Karol opens his eyes, regains his senses. Dominique abruptly unplaits her hair, looks down beneath her. She smiles unpleasantly.

DOMINIQUE

Well?

Karol's eyes are attentive, pleading.

KAROL

I'm sorry . . . Come to Poland with me.

Dominique leans over him, angry now.

DOMINIQUE

I'm not going anywhere with you. I'm going to win all the trials. Divorce, property settlement, everything. You'll leave with your suitcase and diplomas, even though you came with money and a car. Because you never understood a thing and never wanted to understand anything, that's why.

KAROL

I understand . . .

DOMINIQUE
(*shouting*)

You don't understand! You never even tried to understand. If I say I love you, you don't understand. If I say I hate you, you still don't understand! You don't even understand that I want to sleep with you! That I need you. Not even that! Do you understand? No! You're scared of me now, aren't you? Are you scared?

KAROL

I don't know . . .

DOMINIQUE

You don't know . . . You're scared because you don't understand! That's why! Watch this now.

She jumps up. Karol is pressed into the corner of his chair, his hand over his undone flies. Dominique snatches a cigarette lighter from her bag.

Take a good look!

She goes up to the window and sets light to the white, semi-transparent curtain. It immediately bursts into flames.

You broke in and set fire to the place. That's what it'll look like . . .

The heavy blinds catch fire from the curtains.

Soon every cop in Paris will be after you.

Dominique reaches for the telephone and dials a short number. Karol jumps up from where he was sitting, zips up his flies. He grabs his suitcase and roll of diplomas. He runs to the door. The blinds are already on fire.

The keys!

Karol turns round, throws the keys on to the window sill.

EXT. PARIS STREET. DAY

Karol runs another few yards. He stops and turns. Panting, he sees the fire brigade – sirens wailing – and police arrive in front of the hairdressing salon. People are gathering around. Karol turns away, he does not want to watch.

EXT. PARIS STREET. NIGHT

Karol, with several days' stubble, trudges along a well-lit Paris street. He pays no attention to the full restaurants and merry people. Yet something does draw his attention. He walks up to a display. Right by the window, next to shiny old sideboards, tables and lamps, stands an alabaster bust of a woman. Around her head is a wreath of the same material. The woman has a pretty, young face, delicate lips and is looking upwards. Karol stands motionless, his eyes fixed on the bust.

INT. METRO SUBWAY. NIGHT

Karol, his stubble even longer and his face haggard, is sitting in a metro subway, playing on a comb. Next to him lies his open suitcase. There are a few coins and some rolls of paper in it. The metro is quite empty, it is late. Karol puts a lot of heart into the melodious, Polish songs remembered from childhood. People pass by indifferently; music played on a comb is a little too quiet to draw attention. Karol reacts to the sound of a five-franc piece hitting the bottom of his suitcase. He sees a forty-something man who, in passing, throws the coin. Karol reaches for the five-franc piece, blows on it and hides it in his pocket. He plays on. The man's name is Mikołaj. He stops and, from a distance, observes Karol hiding the coin. He turns back and goes up to him. He speaks in Polish.

MIKOŁAJ

May I sit down?

Karol nods in agreement. Mikołaj sits down beside him, tucking his coat underneath him. Karol finishes the melody, pulls the comb away and runs his tongue over his dry lips.

KAROL

How did you guess I was Polish?

Mikołaj smiles.

MIKOŁAJ

I know that song . . .

Karol puts the comb to his lips again and plays a few bars.

KAROL

What about this one?

MIKOŁAJ

I don't like it.

He looks Karol up and down. He speaks casually.

Your flies are undone.

Embarrassed, Karol does the zip up. He avoids eye contact.

KAROL

Sorry . . .

Mikołaj opens his briefcase and pulls out a bottle of whisky. He hands it to Karol and holds out his hand.

MIKOŁAJ

Mikołaj.

KAROL

Karol.

They shake hands and take a sip. Karol obviously likes the whisky.

MIKOŁAJ

Do you live off that comb?

KAROL

I'm trying to. Times are rough . . .

MIKOŁAJ

What's that?

He waves his hand at the rolls of paper in the suitcase. Karol picks up the rolls and spreads them out.

KAROL

Diplomas. I've won competitions . . . Sofia, Budapest, Warsaw . . . They used to be framed, behind glass, but they were too heavy to carry . . .

Mikołaj looks at Karol carefully. He looks through the diplomas.

MIKOŁAJ

Hairdresser?

Karol nods.

Not a bad job.

Karol agrees, a bit surprised by Mikołaj's tone of voice. All of a sudden he yawns dreadfully.

KAROL

Jesuuuus . . . Do you have somewhere to sleep? There's an alcove here . . .

MIKOŁAJ

I do.

He hands the bottle to Karol again. They both sip with pleasure.

Can I sit with you for a bit?

INT. ENTRANCE TO METRO PLATFORM. NIGHT

Karol crosses under the barriers to the platform and waits for Mikołaj.
Mikołaj stops in front of the barrier.

MIKOŁAJ
Wait. I don't like this.

He goes up to the window, hands over some change, the Metro
Employee passes him two tickets. Mikołaj slips the tickets into the
machine and together with Karol, legally, they walk away along the
platform. The last train arrives; nobody gets on and nobody gets off. The
train leaves.

INT. METRO PLATFORM. NIGHT

At the end of the platform, Mikołaj and Karol are in an alcove which
protects them a little from the draught. Other inhabitants of the metro
are also settling down to sleep. The bottle of whisky passing between
Mikołaj's and Karol's hands is already half empty. They are in the
middle of a conversation – the effects of the alcohol are making
themselves felt a bit. Mikołaj pulls out a deck of cards from his briefcase,
rips off the plastic packaging. He shuffles the cards very skilfully and
hands them over to Karol.

MIKOŁAJ
Pick twelve cards.

Karol pulls twelve cards out of the deck. Mikołaj spreads them out,
immediately gathers them and gives them back to Karol.

3, 4, 10, queen of clubs. King of diamonds. Hearts are good:
8, 10, jack, king, ace. Ace and queen of spades.

Karol checks; everything is perfectly correct, although Mikołaj has only
seen the cards for a second.

What counts in bridge is memory. I've played in a good club
for a couple of years, now I'm going home. And you?

KAROL
I want to get out of here . . .

MIKOŁAJ

I'll take you. Tomorrow morning.

Karol shakes his head in disagreement. He speaks with conviction.

KAROL

I kind of doubt it.

He looks at Mikołaj's hair which is slightly too long.

You need a haircut.

Mikołaj nods obediently. Karol pulls out his comb and a pair of thin, silver scissors which he had hidden in the pocket of his jacket. He hands Mikołaj his small mirror with the starlet on the back so that he can keep an eye on the cut. Mikołaj touches the tips of the scissors. They are very sharp.

MIKOŁAJ

Just don't nip me. You've been drinking . . .

KAROL

Don't worry.

Very skilfully, he starts to work on Mikołaj's hair. Meanwhile, he talks.

I've lost my passport. Got no money. The police are after me. No . . . I'm down on my luck. I'll carry on playing here a bit longer, buy a fake passport near the Polish church. Then I'll try . . .

MIKOŁAJ

They're con-men.

KAROL

Con-men . . .

MIKOŁAJ

And not very serious. I offered one of them a good job. He took the money and ran. Maybe you'd like it?

KAROL

Good?

MIKOŁAJ

Very good but unpleasant.

KAROL

I'm a hairdresser.

MIKOŁAJ

Yes. You have to kill someone.

Karol freezes with his scissors, swallows hard. He sits down.

MIKOŁAJ

He wants it done. He doesn't want to go on living and wants help. A fellow Pole. He'll pay well. Enough to live off for six months.

KAROL

Can't you do it?

MIKOŁAJ

It's someone I know. It's got to be a stranger.

KAROL

No . . . No, no. Not that . . . Can't he . . . do it himself?

Mikołaj turns away.

MIKOŁAJ

He wants to, but he can't. He's got a wife and children who love him. Imagine how they'd feel? This way . . . someone kills him . . . these things happen . . .

KAROL

My God . . . He's got a wife, children, money and he wants to kill himself? What am I supposed to say?

No doubt the alcohol is helping to make Karol feel sorry for himself. He shakes Mikołaj by the shoulders, putting the scissors aside.

What am I supposed to say? My wife threw me out with my suitcase and here I am. And I still love her! Even more than before . . . After all she's done to me, I still love her!

There are only two sips of whisky left in the bottle. Mikołaj passes it to Karol. He tips the bottle and drinks what's left. He gurgles, pulls the bottle away from his lips.

MIKOŁAJ

Is she pretty?

KAROL

Beautiful. I first saw her at the Budapest competition . . . A friend was doing her hair. Beautiful. She looked at me . . . Wait, I'll show you.

Karol jumps up, glancing at his watch. Slightly tipsy, he pulls at Mikołaj. They leave the suitcase and scissors and run towards the platform exit.

EXT. PARIS STREET. NIGHT

Karol and Mikołaj emerge from the metro entrance. Karol holds out his hand and points. Opposite the entrance is a large cinema, above it some posters. On a large poster, a photograph of an actress laughing. Mikołaj looks at the poster, carefully following Karol's hand.

MIKOŁAJ

That's her?

Karol nods with a smile.

Michelle Pfeiffer?

Only now does Karol realize what Mikołaj is looking at. He leads Mikołaj's gaze a little to the right, to an apartment window. Lit up from inside it looks cosy.

KAROL

There . . .

A woman's shadow moves and the light goes off.

She's going to sleep.

He watches, moved. He is a little surprised that the light goes on again.

MIKOŁAJ

What's up?

An unsettling shadow moves in the bottom corner of the window.

KAROL

Something's going on.

He makes a move towards the metro, Mikołaj follows. They run down the stairs. A Metro Worker is just locking the metal grille, they run through at the last moment.

INT. ENTRANCE TO THE METRO PLATFORM. NIGHT

Karol runs to a telephone. He rummages in his pocket and pulls out the five-franc piece Mikołaj had given him. In the window, the tired Metro Employee is counting money. Mikołaj, seeing Karol tapping out a telephone number, passes the closed booking office and slips under the barrier on to the platform. Karol listens to the tone. After a moment Dominique answers in a strangely soft voice.

> DOMINIQUE
> *(off)*

Hello . . .

> KAROL

It's me.

> DOMINIQUE
> *(off)*

Perfect timing. Listen.

For a while there is silence, then Karol hears the sound of love-making grow clearer and louder. A man's heavy breathing and Dominique's passionate groans. In the little display window on the telephone his five francs melt away. The number gets smaller and smaller: 4.20, 3.60, 3.20, 2.60.

> KAROL

Dominique, I love you!

But Dominique cannot hear because just at that moment she starts moaning in ecstasy. Karol hangs up violently. In the little window a number has just appeared: 2.20. But the machine does not return his change. Karol wrenches the receiver. He looks around. Runs up to the window where the tired Metro Employee is slogging away at his calculations. This time Karol manages very well in French. He points to the telephone.

> KAROL

It stole two francs!

The tired Metro Employee lifts his head.

Your telephone! It stole two francs.

METRO EMPLOYEE

So what . . .

KAROL

Give it back! Give me back my stolen money!

The Metro Employee finds a two-franc piece among the pile of change, throws it on the revolving tray and pushes it around. Karol grabs the two francs as if his life depended on that coin.

INT. METRO PLATFORM. NIGHT

Karol runs up to the alcove. Mikołaj has fallen asleep, his head on Karol's enormous suitcase. Karol squats down and observes him for a while. A pigeon is sitting right next to Mikołaj's head. For a while, Karol looks it straight in the eyes. Then he notices a lock of Mikołaj's hair sticking out at the side. He finds his scissors. He cuts off the lock of hair, then another one. The pigeon, frightened by the clip of scissors, flies away. Karol smiles at a thought that has just occurred to him. Mikołaj opens an eye. Frightened by the scissors so near his face, he comes to his senses.

KAROL

Take me to Poland. I know how.

MIKOŁAJ

How?

Karol does not answer, suddenly lost in thought.

KAROL

You'll like it. Move your head.

Mikołaj lifts his head from the case. Karol opens it, tips the diplomas out on to the floor. He climbs into the case and arranges himself in a foetal position.

Shut me in.

Mikołaj closes the suitcase. He leans over, hearing a soft scratching. The tip of Karol's scissors appears on one side of the case – a hole is being

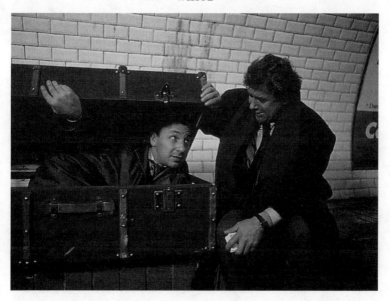

drilled from inside. Mikołaj hears a dull voice coming from within.

> KAROL
> (*off*)
>
> For air. Pick me up.

Mikołaj grabs the handle and lifts the case a couple of inches. He drops it.

> MIKOŁAJ
>
> We'll have to get a trolley, it's heavy. We'll find one at the airport. Can you last out? Three, four hours?

He opens the lid. Karol is lying comfortably inside.

> KAROL
>
> I'll last out. I've just got to do one thing.

> MIKOŁAJ
>
> What?

> KAROL
>
> Steal something.

INT. UNDERGROUND COMPLEX OF PARIS AIRPORT. DAY

Karol's suitcase, secured with a leather belt, travels along the moving pathways of the airport. It travels through low-ceilinged corridors, underground tunnels, constantly changing direction. It falls from a considerable height on to a pile of baggage. An airport Worker grabs it by the handle. He doubles over under its weight, groans.

> WORKER

Shit . . .

With difficulty, helping himself with his knee, he pushes the suitcase on to the trolley. Perhaps through curiosity or maybe for some other reason, he checks the identification tag attached to the handle. He notes something on a slip of paper. The cart emerges from underground.

INT. PARIS AIRPORT. DAY

The trolley travels along the airport tarmac, weaving its way among other trolleys and cars, beneath aeroplane undercarriages. The suitcase wobbles dangerously on the bends, nearly falling off at one point. Placed on a mechanical conveyer belt it majestically disappears into the open hold of a Polish aeroplane.

INT. ARRIVALS HALL, WARSAW AIRPORT. DAY

(Note: from this scene onwards the film takes place entirely in Poland.)

Mikołaj peers into the shabby hole from which emerge suitcases, bundles, boxes tied with string. He grabs a large, soft bag and carries on waiting. Passengers grab hold of their baggage and make their way to customs. There are fewer and fewer people around Mikołaj. With increasing fear, Mikołaj watches the hole which is not spewing out any more baggage. He goes up to a door and pushes it ajar. Beside the trolley, a Man in a Cap is wiping his nose.

> MIKOŁAJ

Is that everything? From Paris?

> MAN IN A CAP

Yes, why?

He is obviously offended by the insinuation that he might have missed

*something. Mikołaj returns to the hall. He walks around, glancing at
the moving empty belt for a while longer, then goes up to a window,
behind which sits a female employee.*

> MIKOŁAJ
> My suitcase's missing. A large case. It's the flight from Paris.

> FEMALE EMPLOYEE
> Your ticket, please.

Mikołaj hands her his ticket. The Employee looks at him attentively.

> What was in the case? Seventy-five kilos?

Mikołaj shuffles uncomfortably from foot to foot.

> MIKOŁAJ
> Personal belongings . . . clothes. To tell the truth, there was a
> man in it.

> FEMALE EMPLOYEE
> A what?

> MIKOŁAJ
> A man. My friend.

EXT. NEAR A RUBBISH DUMP. DUSK

*An enormous rubbish heap where huge garbage trucks look like toys.
Flocks of black birds circle overhead. A delivery van comes to a halt in
some bushes near by. Four men get out, among whom we recognize the
Man in the Cap from the airport. They are all in similar uniforms.
They open the back doors of the van and throw two suitcases out. They
get to work on a third, the heaviest. We know it – it's Karol's enormous
case. Panting, they stand it on the cases they threw out before.*

> MAN IN A CAP
> We'll divide it in five equal parts. Two for me.

> SECOND MAN
> How come?

> MAN IN A CAP
> Handling charges.

The remainder nod their heads, they agree. They cut the belt and smash the locks of the case with a crowbar. They open the lid. Inside, huddled like a baby, lies Karol. In the arch of his bent legs lies the alabaster bust which he had seen in the Paris shop window.

Fuck . . . It's a man.

Karol lifts his head, obviously frightened by the unexpected place in which he now finds himself. He straightens his arms with difficulty.

What the fuck!

Karol, numb with fear, his muscles stiff, tries to climb out of the suitcase. One of the men tips the suitcase, throwing Karol out like a sack of potatoes. The bust falls out with him, rolls down a little further and, hitting a stone, cracks into three parts.

SECOND MAN
Give him here . . .

They lift Karol. One of the men searches him, tears the watch off his wrist.

Made in Russia! The fucking bastard . . .

He throws the watch away and carries on searching. Furious that he has not found a wallet, he punches Karol in the stomach. Something jingles in his trouser pocket. The man shoves his fist down it and pulls it out, triumphantly showing a two-franc piece to the others. He leans over it.

MAN IN A CAP
Two francs. Shit.

Freed from their grip, Karol reaches into the top pocket of his jacket and wrenches out his thin, shiny pair of scissors. He jabs them in the air close to the Man in a Cap's face.

KAROL
Give it back. Come on, give it back!

Attacked like this the Man in a Cap holds out his hand with the coin. Karol, still jabbing with his scissors, takes his two-franc piece. In the meantime, the three remaining men surround him on all sides and, even though Karol tries to defend himself with the scissors, push him over, beat his face and kick him. They stand over Karol, who lies lifelessly.

MAN IN A CAP
Son of a bitch. Fucking beggar.

He kicks Karol again and all four get in the car, throwing the two smaller suitcases in on the way, and leave. Karol lifts his head. His nose is bleeding and his brow is cut. He moans.

KAROL
Jesus . . . Home at last.

EXT. WARSAW STREET. NIGHT

There are still a few wooden houses left among the high tower blocks in this part of Warsaw. Karol, aching and holding on to fences, makes his way with difficulty in the direction of one of them. He drags the case behind him. With surprise, he notices a large sign, 'Karol Hairdressing', lit up from inside. He nearly falls, breaking off the decaying garden gate. He reaches the lit window, and taps on it. Karol's brother Jurek's face appears from inside the room. He looks at Karol as if he were an apparition.

Jesus, Karol . . .

Karol nods, yes it is him. Jurek disappears from the window and runs out of the door. He holds up the falling Karol.

Where did you spring from? What happened?

Karol looks up at the sign.

KAROL
You've got yourself a neon sign . . .

JUREK
A neon, yes. This is Europe, man.

He looks carefully at him and takes him in his arms, hugs him. Karol surrenders to this brotherly hug with pleasure.

INT. HAIRDRESSING SALON. DAY

Jurek finishes washing a middle-aged woman's hair. He puts a towel round her shoulders and walks off when he hears the water boiling.

JUREK

Just a minute, please.

From a metal mug with an electric heating spiral in it, he pours broth into a cup. The Woman's head is tilted back.

MIDDLE-AGED WOMAN

I heard Karol's back?

JUREK

That's right.

He leaves the salon with the cup in his hand.

INT. KAROL'S ROOM. DAY

Jurek, with the cup of broth, enters Karol's room behind the salon. The narrow bed is untidily covered with an eiderdown. Jurek approaches and lifts the eiderdown. Karol is lying there curled up, his knees by his face. He lifts his head at the sight of Jurek.

JUREK

They're asking for you . . .

KAROL

Give me a few more days.

JUREK

Here's some broth.

Karol pulls himself up. Jurek brings the steaming cup to his lips. Karol's lips are swollen. He drinks the broth with difficulty.

EXT. NEAR THE RUBBISH DUMP. DAY

Karol is still moving with difficulty. We see his tiny silhouette against the enormous rubbish heap. He rummages in the grass with his foot, leans over, gets up. He takes a few steps, again parts the grass and the scattered litter with his foot. He squats down, finds a small piece of white alabaster.

INT. KAROL'S ROOM. DAY

Karol carefully applies a layer of glue to a small piece of alabaster. He

*gently fits the missing bit of ear to the already glued female bust. He
presses and holds it in place with his finger for a moment so that the glue
can dry.*

EXT. BY THE RIVER. DUSK

*Karol, juggling the two-franc piece between his fingers, breathes in fresh
air as he walks by the river. He still has a black eye and a swollen brow.
He stops. On the other bank he sees the Old Town and a little to the left –
tall, bright in the setting sun – the tower blocks of the banks and hotels.
Karol looks at them, narrows his eyes, his face sets in an expression of
determination. Abruptly, he throws the coin in the air and catches it. He
holds his clenched fist over the two-franc piece on a level with his face.*

INT. HAIRDRESSING STUDIO. DAY

*In the hairdressing studio Karol – the traces of his beating now barely
visible – skilfully finishes styling a middle-aged woman's hair. Jadwiga,
obviously happy with herself, is looking in the mirror. She speaks
flirtatiously.*

> JADWIGA
> Remember you've got an appointment today.

Karol looks at his watch.

> KAROL
> Thank you.

*He finishes styling and, undoing his apron, makes his way through to
the back rooms. In the small room, containing hairdressing equipment
and a settee, sits Jurek. Seeing Karol standing over him, he reaches for
his wallet.*

> JUREK
> It's payday . . .

He counts out a few hundred thousand zlotys. Through the open door
we see several women waiting to be served. The brother, seeing that
Karol has taken off his apron, waves his hand.*

> You've got clients waiting.

*Translator's note: this is old currency.

KAROL

I can't today. You do them . . .

JUREK

They don't want me any more, not now you're here.

KAROL

Tomorrow then. I'll get up at seven.

Jurek nods all right. Karol puts on his coat and leaves.

EXT. NEAR THE MARRIOTT HOTEL. DAY

There are numerous shabby huts not far from the elegant Marriott hotel. Some sell junk from the Far East, others exchange money. The tall silhouette of the Marriott is impressive. Karol finds the hut he is looking for, watches it for a while. He fiddles in his trouser pocket, takes out his two-franc piece and squeezes it – for luck. He puts it back in his pocket and enters the foreign exchange hut.

INT. FOREIGN EXCHANGE KIOSK. DAY

Karol walks up to the cash desk. The Female Cashier interrupts her crossword with a false smile.

FEMALE CASHIER

How can I help you?

KAROL

I'd like to see the owner . . .

FEMALE CASHIER

Through the back.

The Female Cashier indicates the direction and returns to her crossword. Karol makes his way towards the door. The Female Cashier calls him back.

Do you know the password?

KAROL

No . . .

He comes back and leans over the Cashier. She whispers a few words into his ear. Karol nods.

FEMALE CASHIER

And you've got to push the handle up.

INT./EXT. NEAR THE MARRIOTT HOTEL. DAY

Karol makes his way around the foreign exchange kiosk, jumps over a puddle. Knocking on the door, he throws another glance at the mighty Marriott. The Owner's voice answers from inside.

OWNER
(*off*)

Password?

KAROL

I don't want to.

OWNER
(*off*)

Response?

KAROL

But I have to.

We hear the lock being released.

OWNER

Push the handle up.

Karol enters. The shelves are full of Polish and foreign money. Weighted down, the notes flutter in the draught. The Owner yells.

OWNER

Shut that bloody door!

Karol quickly shuts the door. The Owner counts a pile of money and taps on his calculator.

What is it?

KAROL

I've got an appointment to see you. Jadwiga told me . . .

The Owner nods, that is correct.

OWNER

You do her hair?

KAROL

Yes.

OWNER

Is that all?

He laughs out loud at his joke.

Okay. What do you want?

While talking to Karol, he starts counting another pile of banknotes.

KAROL

I'd like to hang around where there's money. It takes years to get ahead in my line.

OWNER

You're telling me.

He puts the stack of banknotes to one side, feeds the number to his calculator and reaches for yet another bundle. He is an old hand at counting. Karol speaks with pride.

KAROL

I had dealings with banking matters abroad . . . I speak a bit French . . .

The Owner shakes his head. Karol is not sure what he means.

OWNER

We can get on without languages. What we need is trust and expertise. I'd have to try you out . . . I heard how you got out of Paris.

Karol does not deny it. The Owner looks at him attentively for the first time.

You don't particularly stand out. That's good. I need a guard.

He reaches into a drawer and pulls out an enormous gun. He throws it to Karol who, horrified, just about catches it.

OWNER

Relax. It's only tear-gas. Do you have a licence?

KAROL

Come off it.

OWNER

I'll sort one out for you. Hang around outside.

Considering the matter closed, he returns to counting his notes. Karol leaves, taking care to shut the door quickly. Outside, he does not quite know what to do with the weapon. He aims the gun, hides it behind his trouser belt. He walks a few steps away from the exchange kiosk and, in a pretty good frame of mind, stands with his legs apart.

INT. KAROL'S ROOM. NIGHT

In the evening Karol makes himself something to drink in the back room of his brother's hairdressing studio. He takes the heating spiral out of the mug and pours a spoonful of tea-leaves into the boiling water. He stirs it with a spoon so that the leaves fall to the bottom. The settee is already made up as a bed, on the linen lies the huge gun. A small lamp is on. Sipping his drink, with his eyes closed, Karol is repeating French vocabulary to himself. He checks in the textbook and, trying to repeat the words with a correct accent, switches on the tape recorder. He is doing pretty well. After a while he loses the thread, stops repeating and then the tape recorder conjugates subsequent verbs by itself. Karol gazes somewhere in front of him. On a shelf stands the alabaster bust, now neatly glued together. Karol does not take his eyes off it. The tape recorded repeats vocabulary. Karol gets up and approaches the bust. Suddenly he leans over and gives the woman's lips a long, delicate kiss. He closes his eyes.

INT. BATHROOM IN JUREK'S HOUSE. DAY

Karol in the bathroom, holding a cut-throat razor in his hand, turns as he hears a knock on the door. He has just shaved half of his face, the rest is covered in soap.

KAROL

One moment!

The knocking continues, more energetically. Karol opens the door. In the doorway stands Jurek.

Come in.

JUREK

No. I just . . . Are you happy here?

KAROL

In the bathroom?

JUREK

No, in general.

KAROL

Yes, I am.

JUREK

You can stay if you like. But we've got to settle things.

Karol wipes the soap off the remaining half of his face.

KAROL

I can pay you.

JUREK

No, it's not that. I'd like you to do some hair. Ten heads a week, let's say. They want you.

KAROL

Five.

JUREK

Okay, seven.

KAROL

Seven.

Jurek holds out his open hand to clinch the deal. Karol holds out his, transferring the razor into his left hand.

JUREK

Someone was looking for you. Fortyish, not very tall. Sad-looking . . .

KAROL

That's Mikołaj. He brought me back from Paris.

JUREK

He was glad to know you're alive.

KAROL

Did he leave his phone number?

JUREK

No, nothing. He just said to say 'Hi' and left.

KAROL

'Hi' . . . Pity.

INT. FOREIGN EXCHANGE KIOSK. DAY

The Female Cashier checks two hundred-dollar banknotes carefully before handing over a wad of Polish notes. She glances at Karol who is standing in the corner indicating 'everything's fine'. Karol nods – 'I'm here if you need me' – and goes outside.

EXT. NEAR THE MARRIOTT HOTEL. DAY

It is cold outside. Karol pulls his trousers up a little so as not to get them muddy. He looks around. A Tall Man standing motionless draws his attention. Karol, pretending he couldn't care less, walks round the exchange kiosk and carefully creeps around the corner. The Tall Man, obviously watching the kiosk, does not move from the spot. Karol crosses the street, peeps out from behind a post. The Tall Man has changed position, but only lights a cigarette and continues to watch carefully. Karol stiffens, touches the place where he usually carries his gun. He goes back to the kiosk and walks around it so as to get to the entrance from the back. He knocks on the door, the Owner appears.

KAROL

Someone's watching us.

OWNER

Let him.

KAROL

A big guy. He hasn't moved from the spot.

The owner follows Karol unwillingly. They emerge from around the corner, Karol points to the Tall Man. The Owner immediately turns his back. He hisses furiously.

> OWNER

Hide me. Hide me!

Karol obeys with difficulty; he is much shorter than his boss.

We're going back.

Trying to cover the Owner, Karol retreats to the back room of the kiosk. They go inside.

INT. FOREIGN EXCHANGE KIOSK. DAY

Closing the door, the Owner looks at his watch.

> OWNER

Oh, shit. It's three already.

He immediately makes a decision.

Hurry to the crossroads, 500 yards from here. A blue Volkswagen will be coming from Mokotów. Stop it even if it runs you down. Don't let it come here. Make it go to the Ambassador café. Hurry!

The Owner shoves Karol out and watches through the office window to see if he will make it.

EXT. CROSSROADS. DAY

Karol runs up to the crossroads. He sees the Volkswagen approaching. He gathers speed, panting for breath. He tears across the middle of the crossroads, unfortunately the Volkswagen has just passed a green light. Karol rushes straight into the car with arms outspread. At the last moment the car brakes with a screech of tyres. Inside sits a thirty-year-old Blonde, pale with terror. She lowers her window when the panting, and equally terrified, Karol approaches the car.

> KAROL

The boss has asked you to go to the Ambassador café.

The Blonde smiles pleasantly, innocently.

                BLONDE

The Ambassador . . . okay. Are you coming with me?

                KAROL

I've got to get back.

                BLONDE

Would you like a lift?

Karol protests vehemently.

                KAROL

God forbid! Don't even go near the exchange kiosk!

He watches the Blonde close her window and drive away, turning to the right.

EXT. NEAR THE MARRIOTT HOTEL. DAY

Karol, stumbling from the exertion, returns to the exchange kiosk. The Tall Man is still standing at his post. The Owner is waiting in the door.

                KAROL

I made it.

                OWNER

Good. Now get rid of him.

                KAROL

How?

                OWNER

Get him out of my sight for a moment. That's what you're paid for.

Karol only takes a second to think it over.

                KAROL

Give me a cigarette.

The Owner pulls out a packet of Marlboros and hands it to Karol.

One.

He carefully takes out one cigarette from the packet.

With the cigarette in his mouth, he approaches the Tall Man.

Have you got a light?

The Tall Man has to turn his back to the exchange kiosk for a moment to light Karol's cigarette. Karol evidently exaggerates the lighting up of his cigarette. He shelters the flame with his hands, leans over again pretending that the cigarette did not light the first time and finally inhales with pleasure.

(*politely*)

Thank you very much.

Without moving from the spot he continues.

What are you hanging around here for?

The Tall Man is furious.

TALL MAN

This is a democracy. I can stand where I like.

KAROL

Yes. But I'm guarding big money and you've been hanging around here since morning.

TALL MAN

Fuck off. Or I'll hit you.

And suddenly he stretches his huge hands towards Karol's neck. Karol jumps aside and reaches for his gun. Behind the Tall Man's back he sees the Owner getting into his car and, looking back to make sure he has not been noticed, drive away. The Tall Man stands up straight.

Shoot then. Go on, shoot!

Karol abandons the idea of taking out his gun. He spits out the lit cigarette and with feigned pride walks away. After a moment, he stops. He knows that the Tall Man watching the exchange kiosk has his eye on him all the time. He turns back and, without hurrying, crosses the square and goes up to the Tall Man again. He stands next to him not saying anything. The Tall Man looks at him, not understanding his intentions. They stand like that for a while in silence.

What's up?

KAROL

You might as well go. There's no point in standing around.

He speaks seriously and amicably. The Tall Man notices this.

TALL MAN

She's not coming?

KAROL

No.

TALL MAN

And him? He's gone?

KAROL

Yes.

The Tall Man sighs deeply and turns his back on Karol. After a moment, Karol gently touches his shoulder.

Excuse me . . .

The Tall Man turns around. He looks hurt.

Don't come here any more.

TALL MAN

Not come?

KAROL

No. Why know everything?

The Tall Man nods, yes, Karol is right.

INT. KAROL'S ROOM. NIGHT

In the evening, Karol turns on the lamp in his room. Without taking off his coat, he pulls out his suitcase from under the bed. There is a cardboard box inside. In the box, under several shirts, is a shoe box. Karol opens it and adds another wad of money to the wads already there. His face is determined. He hears a rustling, something distinctly hits the window. Karol immediately closes the box, covers it with his whole body. He looks towards the window. The knocking is not repeated. Karol, covering the box, hides it under his bed. Slowly, he approaches the window. He screens his eyes with his hand. After a while, he makes out a dove. Regaining her balance, the dove makes herself comfortable in the nest she has made in the curve of the roof. Flapping her wings, she carefully sits on two small eggs. Karol observes her with the fascination of someone who never pays any attention to nature. The dove settles quite comfortably in her nest and looks attentively straight at Karol.

EXT. NEAR WARSAW. DAY

At dawn, a powerful yet inconspicuous Mercedes takes the northern road out of Warsaw. The Owner of the exchange kiosk is driving and next to him sits an elegant man with a rather coarse face. They are talking quietly, only scraps of their conversation reach us.

OWNER

In Gdańsk we'll exchange at thirty . . . In Toruń . . . in the
Investment Bank . . . You'll get credit . . .

DANDY

How much?

OWNER

Let's say two hundred . . . transfer the credit . . . The
percentage is lower . . . in the Trade Bank . . .

DANDY

Pretty smart.

OWNER

Only seven per cent. But if we triple the rate . . .

DANDY

Do you remember where it was?

The Owner says yes. Karol is asleep in the back, squeezing two large briefcases under his arm. They drive through the suburbs, peasant dwellings, fences. The Dandy glances back, notices that Karol is asleep and nods. The Owner very carefully stops the car at the roadside.

OWNER

Is he asleep?

The Dandy confirms this. They get out trying not to make a noise. Karol opens an eye for a moment. The Dandy shows the Owner a site cut off on the horizon by a river slope, he waves his arms around.

> DANDY
>
> This is where Hartwig and Ikea want to build their warehouses. And these . . .

He nods towards some buildings.

> They're dumb and don't know anything. No one does. And I'm not breathing a word. Thirty per cent profit.

The Owner nods in agreement.

> OWNER
>
> We'll talk when it's confirmed.

> DANDY
>
> Okay.

They both nod, the matter is clear. They go back to the car. The Owner, pleased, slams the door and shouts to Karol.

> OWNER
>
> Wake up! Don't sleep! They'll steal you!

Karol jumps, touches both briefcases. The Owner smiles, the joke worked. The car moves off, leaves the place. The Owner and the Dandy again plunge into an uninteresting, financial conversation.

> DANDY
>
> Are they prepared?

> OWNER
>
> Yes . . . what do you think? I've been dealing with them for three years . . .

Karol discreetly pulls out a piece of paper and, glancing at a passing signpost with the name of the place, notes down the name – we do not know why.

INT. EXCHANGE KIOSK. DUSK

There's nobody in the exchange kiosk at the end of the day. The Female Cashier locks the till and starts getting dressed when Karol appears in the door. He approaches the window, smiles.

KAROL

Can you exchange this for me, Eve?

The Female Cashier smiles, too, and reopens the till. Karol pulls out the shoe box from under his jacket and opens it. He lays out several rather large bundles of various banknotes. The Female Cashier steals a glance, curious.

FEMALE CASHIER

You've collected quite a bit . . .

Karol is slightly embarrassed.

KAROL

I work.

He looks on with pleasure as the Female Cashier starts to count his money with professional skill.

INT. OFF-LICENCE. DUSK

Several people queue in the off-licence. Karol, reaching the counter, stands a new leather briefcase on it.

KAROL

A bottle of vodka, please. The best.

The Female Shop Assistant hands him a decent-looking bottle.

Wrap it up, please.

Carefully, he puts the bottle, wrapped in paper, inside his new briefcase.

EXT. IN FRONT OF THE OFF-LICENCE. DUSK

Karol leaves the shop and tries to cross the street as quickly as possible. He is held to the spot by a terrifying hooting of a car. He looks around, frightened. The Blonde waves to him from a parked blue Volkswagen. Karol approaches.

BLONDE

Good evening. Don't you recognize me?

KAROL

Of course I do.

BLONDE

You did a good deed.

Karol does not trust her much.

KAROL

What?

BLONDE

You said something to my husband. I don't know what . . .

KAROL

Maybe . . .

BLONDE

He's calmed down a bit.

She gets out of the car, slams the door.

KAROL

How's that?

BLONDE

He's jealous . . . But now he's realized that I've got my own
affairs and he's got to come to terms with it.

KAROL

I'm glad.

BLONDE

What clever thing did you say to him?

KAROL

I don't remember.

*The Blonde holds out her hand in goodbye. Karol, despite himself, kisses
it. The Blonde does not let go of his hand.*

BLONDE

What did you buy?

KAROL

Polonez.

BLONDE

Would you like to drink it with me? I've got a free evening

WHITE

. . . We could have breakfast in the morning . . .

Karol swallows nervously.

KAROL

Thanks a lot . . . I'm in a hurry.

The Blonde lets go of his hand.

BLONDE

You'll regret it.

KAROL

I kind of doubt it.

He runs across the street and turns in the direction of the Śródmieście railway station.

The Blonde smiles to herself seeing his small, disappearing figure.

EXT. NEAR WARSAW. DUSK

Karol emerges from a peasant's cottage. We recognize the site – buildings, fences, river slope. A Peasant explains something to Karol as he shows him the direction. Karol, with his new briefcase, walks up to a cottage standing on its own. He knocks. He smiles as pleasantly as he can when the door opens. An Old Peasant looks at him suspiciously.

KAROL

Can I come in? I'm here on business.

The Old Peasant measures him up and down without opening the door any further.

OLD PEASANT

Official?

Karol opens his leather suitcase and takes out the wrapped bottle of vodka. He unwraps the paper. Suspicion does not disappear from the Old Peasant's face. Karol reveals quite a large packet of dollars in the briefcase.

KAROL

No, I wanted to talk business.

147

INT. THE COTTAGE. NIGHT

The Old Peasant pours them half a glass of vodka each. They must have already had a number of drinks because he drains the bottle carefully, so as not to miss a single drop. Some papers, plans and an agreement obviously drawn up on the spot lie spread out on the table. They clink glasses and, with one gulp, knock back their half-glassfuls. The Old Peasant picks up a pen, gets ready to sign. He holds the pen over where he is to sign, then puts it aside resolutely and screws on the lid. Karol sighs.

OLD PEASANT

What's it to you?

KAROL

I've already told you.

OLD PEASANT

Tell me again. I like hearing it.

KAROL

I'll build myself a summer house here. A cottage and a piece of land, that's all. The rest will stay as it is. You can stay put, rent out or sell.

OLD PEASANT

Yes . . .

He unscrews the pen again, but does not get ready to sign. Karol looks on anxiously.

You're right, it's not far from town. So many people are hanging around . . . Maybe it's some sort of special land? What?

KAROL

But you wanted to visit your son . . .

OLD PEASANT

So I did.

KAROL

You'll visit your son. Buy a car, TV . . .

148

OLD PEASANT

What for? I never watch. It's silly. Unless I shove it in the ground, put it in a jar and bury it. I could do that, couldn't I?

KAROL

Sure.

OLD PEASANT

That would be nice.

The Old Peasant suddenly signs the document decisively. Karol breathes a sigh of relief. He hands the Old Peasant the wad of dollars.

KAROL

There's a thousand here. Deposit. I'll give you four thousand in a month's time, when we close the deal.

The Old Peasant counts the money very slowly. Karol stretches himself.

I have to go. It's the last train.

OLD PEASANT

Are you going to go wandering around at night? You'll get mugged, they'll steal your briefcase . . . Sleep here.

Karol is glad of the offer.

KAROL

Here?

OLD PEASANT

Here. There's a bed upstairs.

The Old Peasant takes Karol to a little attic room. There is a pleasant old bed there. Karol sits on it with force. The thick duvet gives way.

OLD PEASANT

It's yours now.

INT./EXT. COTTAGE. DAY

Karol wakes at dawn dressed in his vest. He opens the window. Outside the Old Peasant is carefully counting steps and hammering posts into the ground which, from now, will belong to Karol. There is not much of it, 100, maybe 200 square yards, but Karol, seeing the posts knocked well into the ground, smiles. He reaches for his comb and little mirror and arranges his hair. This time he combs it right back, as if trying out a new hairstyle. It looks good, but Karol returns to the old style. He is obviously in a good mood.

INT./EXT. NEAR THE MARRIOTT HOTEL. DUSK

Karol routinely walks around his exchange kiosk. He stiffens when he hears a cry from inside: 'It's a raid! Hands up!' Through the window he sees two clients hesitantly putting their hands up. The Female Cashier's face flashes by – it looks as if she is smiling. Karol pulls out his gun, in two jumps is at the door, kicks it in and, bursting in, shoots gas at an elegantly dressed man who is standing with his back to him. All this lasts a few seconds. The guy, stupefied by the gas, doubles over, coils up, falls on his knees sheltering and rubbing his eyes. The Owner bursts in from behind the curtain. He leans over the crawling guy, trying to help him get up. He shouts to Karol at the same time.

OWNER

Are you crazy? Don't you recognize people you know?

It is only now that Karol recognizes the crude face of the Dandy. Tears are rolling down his face, his nose is red and swollen. Karol stutters with agitation.

KAROL

Sorry . . . maybe I'll . . . maybe I'll . . . call a doctor. Phone.

The Owner takes the Dandy through the narrow door to the back room. He stops Karol, who is getting ready to phone.

OWNER

Leave it!

Karol tries to help move the injured man, but the Owner resolutely tears the Dandy away from him.

You're lucky it was from the back. That idiot would've burnt your eyes out . . .

Karol staggers out on wobbly legs. He gasps for fresh air. Weak, he leans against the wooden wall of the exchange kiosk. The Dandy's

*moans and the Owner's words of comfort reach him. Karol brings his
ear closer to the wall. He hears the Dandy's voice with traces of tears
and mucus caused by the gas.*

DANDY
(*off*)

They've outbid us. Some son of a bitch has outbid us . . .

OWNER
(*off*)

Who?

DANDY
(*off*)

I don't know. But I'll find out. Our only chance now is that
he won't make the payments on time . . .

*Karol tears his ear away from the wooden wall. He is evidently
frightened by what he hears. Feverishly, he looks for a solution. He
makes a decision.*

EXT. TELEPHONE BOX. DAY

*Karol flicks through a telephone directory in the phone box. Tattered
pages, a smoking fag end. Karol does not enjoy stubbing it out. He finds
the right page in the book. He runs his finger down the line of addresses
and stops at the place he needs. It is the address of an institution on
Nowy Świat Street. Karol memorizes the number.*

EXT. NOWY ŚWIAT STREET. DAY

*Karol walks down the street looking at the descending numbers. He
reaches the right one but does not find the name of the institution he is
looking for on the signboard. He takes a step back into the street to look
at the whole house. On the first-floor balcony, he notices two middle-
aged women talking, perplexed by something.*

KAROL

Excuse me . . .

The Women interrupt their conversation, look in his direction.

I'm looking for the Polish Association of Sports Bridge.

WOMAN

That's here.

Karol, pleased, thanks them with a wave of the hand. He asks out of politeness.

KAROL

May I?

The Woman motions her hand to say no.

WOMAN

What do you want? We've got elections at the moment . . .

KAROL

I'm looking for an eminent bridge player. Mikołaj. About forty, average height . . .

The Woman interrupts him. She knows Mikołaj and probably does not like him much.

WOMAN

Mikołaj? He's not here. He doesn't take part in the Association's activities.

KAROL

Do you know where I can find him? His address or telephone number . . .

WOMAN

There's a match with the Germans in three days' time. He's going to be playing.

EXT. NEAR THE MARRIOTT HOTEL. DAY

In the morning, Karol nears the exchange kiosk with resolute determination. The sight of a blue Volkswagen parked in front of the kiosk stops him. Karol knocks on the back door. He opens, hearing someone call from inside: 'Come in!'

INT. FOREIGN EXCHANGE KIOSK. DAY

He stops at the threshold. Inside are the Owner, the Blonde and the Tall Man. They are all laughing at a joke which the Owner has evidently just finished telling. The Tall Man keeps his distance. Karol wants to back away.

KAROL

Sorry . . .

OWNER

Come in, come in, don't be embarrassed.

KAROL

Maybe later.

OWNER

Come in. What can I do for you?

Karol wants to leave.

BLONDE

You're going to lose something.

KAROL

I'm sorry?

BLONDE

Your flies . . .

Karol zips up his flies.

KAROL
(*resolutely*)

I want to quit, boss.

OWNER

Quite right. You know too much anyway.

Karol pulls out his huge gun and places it on the table. The Owner pushes it towards the Tall Man who picks the gun up unwillingly. Karol watches the three of them with astonishment. The Tall Man lowers his eyes.

OWNER

And the arms licence.

Karol reaches for his wallet, but stops halfway.

KAROL
(*resolutely*)
Not the licence. The licence is in my name. It's mine.

INT. SPORTS HALL. DAY

Several tables covered with green baize have been arranged in the middle of the hall. At them sit bridge players. Spectators wander around. The stands, now empty, disappear upwards into the darkness. Karol walks around among the spectators looking carefully at the players. At the last table, he catches sight of Mikołaj. He is playing his cards. He plays quickly and, without particular pleasure, collects trick after trick. He waits for his opponents' discards impatiently. During one such interval, he feels Karol's eyes on him. He raises his eyes and winks. Karol smiles. Mikołaj finishes the game, taking the last trick. He gets up.

MIKOŁAJ
Thank you. *Danke schön.*

He walks up to Karol and greets him. He takes him aside between the rows of the stands.

KAROL
You played beautifully.

MIKOŁAJ
It's easy with the Germans. I've been looking for you . . .

He looks at him carefully, smiles.

KAROL
Me too.

MIKOŁAJ
You're alive.

KAROL
They stole me with the case.

MIKOŁAJ
I know. Your brother told me.

The conversation suddenly dries up. However, Mikołaj feels that Karol has something to ask him but feels awkward about bringing it up. He encourages Karol, smiles.

What's up?

KAROL

You mentioned a guy, in the metro . . . d'you remember?

MIKOŁAJ

Yes.

KAROL

Are you in touch with him? Could you call?

Mikołaj, surprised, scrutinizes Karol.

MIKOŁAJ

Yes, I could . . .

Karol looks at him calmly.

KAROL

If a man needs help, he needs help, right?

Now Mikołaj clearly understands what Karol means. A moment's silence.

MIKOŁAJ

Except he's back in Warsaw.

Disappointed, Karol nods.

KAROL

Doesn't want to any more . . .

Mikołaj does not change his tone.

MIKOŁAJ

On the contrary. He does. More than ever.

INT. KAROL'S ROOM. NIGHT

A round object, flicked by a finger, is spinning around on a table in the back room of the hairdressing salon. It traces small circles, but does not reach the French dictionary and exercise book full of vocabulary which are spread out there. The movement slows down and after some time we recognize the object – it is a coin. It makes one more small circle and falls. Karol, who set it spinning, is sitting at the table. The two-franc coin falls just by his finger. Karol covers it with his palm and then slowly uncovers it to see what's face up – heads or tails. It is tails. Karol sighs, gets up and walks up to the alabaster bust of the woman. He gently touches the base of the nose with his finger. He strokes the place for a moment.

EXT. NEAR THE RUBBISH DUMP. DUSK

Wasteland near the rubbish dump. We now see the heap of rubbish with its black birds from a different perspective. Karol has sat down on the bumper of a rusty, long-deserted car. All around are bushes, car wrecks, old tyres, muddy holes in the earth. Karol waits. It is growing dark. He hears the sound of someone approaching. He gets up. A man, coming up the hill from the direction of the town, is coming closer. Only when he is near does Karol recognize Mikołaj. They shake hands.

MIKOŁAJ

Good place . . .

KAROL

So, he's changed his mind?

MIKOŁAJ

No. It's me.

KAROL

Christ almighty . . .

MIKOŁAJ

Does it make a difference?

KAROL

No . . . But it's you.

MIKOŁAJ

So what, I'm not human?

KAROL

You're human.

156

MIKOŁAJ

Well. The envelope's in my pocket. You can take it afterwards. Here?

Karol confirms this and Mikołaj, cutting short the conversation, makes the first move towards the darkening bushes. Karol catches him up, they walk side by side. Suddenly Karol stops. So does Mikołaj. He looks questioningly.

KAROL

It's neither here nor there . . . But why?

MIKOŁAJ

You're right. It's neither here nor there.

He moves forward. After a few steps, Karol stops, pulls out a gun.

KAROL
(*quietly*)

Mikołaj.

Mikołaj turns and now sees Karol with the gun in his hand. Karol slowly moves in, holding the gun at the level of Mikołaj's heart. He stops just in front of him. He looks him in the eyes.

Are you sure?

Mikołaj closes his eyes, clearly meaning: yes. Karol pulls the trigger. The noise is quite loud. Mikołaj slowly sinks to the ground just by Karol's legs. Karol leans over him, looks closely at the calm face. After a long while, Mikołaj opens his eyes. He does not know where he is, cannot believe that he sees Karol's face over him.

That was a blank. The next one's real.

He shows Mikołaj the bullet. He loads it into the cylinder, the grating of metal. Mikołaj does not move. Karol aims the gun right up against his heart.

Are you sure?

This time Mikołaj does not close his eyes. Karol waits for the sign.

(*irritated, louder*)

Are you sure?

Mikołaj answers only after a long, tense moment.

MIKOŁAJ

No.

He holds out his hand and Karol pulls him up. Mikołaj is shaking a little, Karol supports him.

Not any more.

KAROL

Are you going to tell me why?

MIKOŁAJ

I don't know how to put it . . . I was suffering.

KAROL

Everyone suffers.

MIKOŁAJ

Yes. But I wanted less of it.

He reaches into his pocket and pulls out the envelope.

The deal stands.

Karol hesitates for a moment.

You've earned it. Really.

KAROL

I did earn it, but I'm only borrowing it.

MIKOŁAJ

Okay.

Karol takes the envelope and hides it in his pocket. Suddenly he grows weak and would probably collapse if it was not for Mikołaj. They both squat down.

KAROL

Oh, my God . . .

MIKOŁAJ

How about a drink?

Karol raises his eyebrows. A drink.

EXT. BY THE RIVER. DAWN

The Vistula is very high and has frozen over in the middle of town, even though it is not snowing yet. A yellowish, winter sun rises. The contours of Warsaw with the Old Town and Palace of Culture, a fisherman holding a rod in a hole in the ice. Karol picks up speed and, just about keeping his balance, takes a long slide along the smooth ice. Behind him Mikołaj takes off with what remains of their bottle of whisky. He has obviously taken a better run because he catches up with Karol. They tumble down on the ice together. Laughing, they lie looking at the rising sun.

MIKOŁAJ

Christ . . . I feel just like a kid again.

KAROL

So do I.

MIKOŁAJ

Everything's possible.

INT. KAROL'S ROOM, HAIRDRESSING SALON. DAY

Karol is woken at dawn by a hammering on the salon door. He gets up from bed, glancing at the alarm clock – it is six in the morning. Grunting, half asleep, frozen, he opens the door. There is snow outside, a long time must have passed since the last scene. The Owner and the Dandy, smartly dressed as always, stand at the door. They do not appear friendly. Karol winces in his underpants and vest – it does not look as if he can stand up to them. They enter uninvited and slam the door. They shove Karol into the hairdressing salon. The Dandy speaks with concern.

DANDY

You beat us to it. You bought the land.

He suddenly throws himself at Karol and squeezes his neck with the straps of his vest. The Owner doesn't want to get his hands dirty – he merely comes closer.

You spied, you bastard.

He squeezes tighter.

159

KAROL

I did . . .

DANDY

I'm going to strangle you.

He squeezes even tighter and it is obvious that he is not joking. Karol wheezes with the greatest difficulty, losing his breath.

KAROL

I've got a will . . . And it's airtight . . .

The Owner watches him attentively, nudges the Dandy, who loosens his grip. Karol regains his breath, gasps greedily.

I've made sure it's airtight.

OWNER

What do you mean 'airtight'?

KAROL

Just in case . . . Everything goes to the Church.

The Owner sits on one of the hairdressing chairs. He wipes his forehead.

OWNER

Oh Christ, the Church. We're screwed.

Karol agrees with that. The Owner waves to the Dandy.

Let him go.

The Dandy lets Karol go, pushes him as if lightly, but Karol only comes to a halt when he reaches the iron stove some few yards away.

You're lucky it's not on . . .

The Dandy sits next to him on a low stool. He mutters something to himself; Karol, in no state to hear, picks himself up from under the stove. The Dandy comes up to him. Karol instinctively backs away, but the Dandy only brushes him down and draws a hairdressing chair up to him. Karol keeps on trembling from cold and fear.

Sorry, we went too far. Let's talk?

Karol has nothing against it.

Will you sell?

KAROL

I will.

OWNER

Good . . .

He reflects seriously then suddenly asks.

How much?

KAROL

Ten times what I paid. Fifty thousand dollars.

The Owner nods, this is what he expected. The nod is not just an agreement to the sum but a nod as to the wretchedness of this world and his own stupidity.

Excuse me while I get changed.

He leaves the place. Jurek is standing in the hall with a bucket full of coal and wood for fuel.

> **JUREK**

What the hell is going on?

Karol smiles.

> **KAROL**

It's okay. I'll be able to pay you back.

He disappears from the room, pulls on his trousers and jacket over his vest and drags his suitcase from under the bed. He pulls out a map from it. Jurek appears at the door.

> **JUREK**

Shall I light the stove?

Karol runs past him with the map in his hand.

> **KAROL**

Later . . .

He goes into the salon, closes the door. He spreads the map out on the floor. It is long, stuck together in several places, and covers the strip of land between the road and river. Small squares have been marked in a few places with a red felt-tip pen. Karol shows these places to his guests.

This may interest you . . . I've also got a plot here. Here and here . . . And here, too.

> **OWNER**

Shit. Everything's right in the middle.

> **KAROL**

Exactly.

He points to one of the squares.

I couldn't resist this one. Beautiful spot. Birch saplings . . .

> **OWNER**

Which means?

> **KAROL**

Same. Ten times as much. It's exceptional land. I've got everything. Bills, contracts . . . That's the way it is. For the time being.

Emphasizing 'for the time being', he spreads his arms out helplessly.

OWNER

A pile of money.

KAROL

You'll make it up.

OWNER

It's a deal.

He holds his hand out to Karol. Karol shakes it, the Owner squeezes hard, brings his face up to Karol.

(*quietly*)

You're one son of a bitch.

Karol answers calmly, looking him in the eyes.

KAROL

No. I just need the money.

Jurek stands in the doorway with a bucket in his hand.

JUREK

Excuse me, shall I light the stove?

The Owner lets go of Karol's hand.

KAROL

Yes. It's cold.

JUREK

Maybe you could . . . Jadwiga asked whether you could do her hair today?

KAROL

Today? Why not?! I've got a bit of time.

EXT. IN FRONT OF MIKOŁAJ'S HOUSE. DAY

It is still winter. A neighbourhood of decently built pre-fab family houses. From the back seat of a car, Karol watches the entry to a little street. He is dressed in a suit, his hair slicked back. He has changed. He is warm and comfortable. At the wheel sits Bronek, the chauffeur. He is a serious fifty-year-old. He turns to Karol.

163

> BRONEK

Shall I turn the engine off, boss?

> KAROL

No, keep the car warm, Bronek.

He notices Mikołaj's Japanese car drive into the estate. He waits a moment longer. Mikołaj takes several rather large packages out of the boot. Karol gets out, they greet each other. We can see that they meet from time to time and like each other. Mikołaj is in a good mood, smiling.

Shopping . . .

> MIKOŁAJ

Presents . . . Are you coming in? They'll be pleased to see you.

> KAROL

No. I'll just be a second.

Mikołaj puts the presents aside for a moment. It is obvious that this is serious.

> MIKOŁAJ

Yes?

> KAROL

I'm starting a company. Big time. Thirty per cent of the capital comes from the money you gave me.

> MIKOŁAJ

You know your way around.

> KAROL

Like it or not you're my partner. I'd like you to run it with me.

> MIKOŁAJ

Seriously?

> KAROL

Seriously.

Mikołaj looks at the shining Volvo. A fine thread of smoke streams from the exhaust pipe. Bronek gets out and cleans the rear lights.

MIKOŁAJ

Yours?

KAROL

Company's. On expenses.

MIKOŁAJ

Give me a bit of time to think it over.

KAROL

Sure.

Karol turns around, hearing the quiet sound of a little bell. A black car, adorned with wreaths, emerges from the gate of a house near by. An altar boy, ringing the little bell, and a priest follow the car. Then several people in dark coats. They get into a parked bus. Karol watches this short picture with incredible attention.

INT. OFFICES IN THE MARRIOTT HOTEL. DAY

The doors of several elegant offices in the Marriott hotel are wide open. Karol and Mikołaj, in the company of an attractive Manager, are looking around the premises. The Manager is giving them a spiel on what she is selling. She has got a cold and sneezes elegantly into a paper hankie. She points out the large windows with a view of the Palace of Culture and the Central Station, the possibility of moving the walls and arranging the furniture. The floor shines. The Manager walks up to one of the walls. There are a number of sockets of different sizes.

MANAGER

Computer and satellite hook-ups.

KAROL

And fax? We need two. Where do we plug them in?

MANAGER

You've got three telephone lines here.

KAROL

Oh, into the phone . . .

MANAGER

Yes. Will you step into my office?

KAROL

Yes, in a minute. I think we'll take everything.

He points to both the executive's and the secretary's offices. The Manager leaves. Karol stops her.

May I have a tissue? A tissue . . .

The Manager takes out a clean tissue from her little packet. She leaves. Karol pulls his comb out from his top pocket. He looks out of the window.

Nice. Warsaw at our feet.

MIKOŁAJ

Nice.

Karol places the tissue on his comb and starts playing the melody from the metro.

KAROL

You like it?

Mikołaj nods. Karol continues playing for a while.

EXT. ENTRANCE TO THE MARRIOTT HOTEL. DUSK

There is no snow outside any more. Karol leaves through the main, grand hotel entrance. He walks up to his parked Volvo. He slams the door with force. He turns on the motor. As he turns to reverse someone opens his door. A nervous Young Man. Next to him another equally nervous Young Man.

KAROL

Yes?

Both Young Men are breathing quickly. They speak in French.

YOUNG MAN I

Do you speak French?

Karol replies in perfectly correct French.

KAROL

Yes.

YOUNG MAN I

Have you seen . . . we just parked our car here a moment ago
. . . Now it's gone.

KAROL

No, I haven't.

YOUNG MAN 2

Someone's pinched it. With our passports, money,
everything.

KAROL

That's a hassle. Are you from France?

YOUNG MAN 2

Switzerland. But we're on our way to England. We've got to
call the police.

KAROL

Yes. But that won't get you anywhere. It's the embassy you
want, but it's too late today. You've got to sleep somewhere.

The Young Men only now realize the full gravity of their situation.

YOUNG MAN I

We haven't got our passports. And no money.

KAROL

I can see that. I can't offer you my place because I haven't got
one myself. But you can doss down in my office. Here.

He points to the silhouette of the Marriott.

INT. CORRIDOR AND OFFICE IN THE MARRIOTT. NIGHT

*Karol, with the two frightened, sympathetic Swiss, steps out of the large
lift. They finish the conversation they had started in the lift.*

KAROL

What are you doing in Poland?

YOUNG MAN I

Economics of what used to be Communist countries.

KAROL

Interesting subject.

Karol leads them along the corridor and opens the office. Everything is now arranged with pretty good taste. Computers, desks, faxes, telephones, armchairs. Karol invites his guests into the executive office. He shows them two large, leather couches.

You can sleep here. It's warm, but just in case . . .

He takes a blanket out of a cupboard and throws it to the boys.

Feel free to send a fax if you need to. They're both working.

He checks the 'on' lights of both faxes.

I'll ask my chauffeur to drive you to the embassy tomorrow morning. Goodnight.

INT. WAREHOUSE. NIGHT

Karol is asleep in a small packing-room at the back of an enormous warehouse.

The packing-room is not large. There is a bed, telephone, fax, several of Karol's suits hanging on nails, the alabaster bust on a shelf. Karol is sleeping peacefully, but he wakes up suddenly and sits up in bed in a cold sweat. A strange light falls through the little window illuminating the warehouse and the bust. Karol looks at this light with unease. He wipes his forehead. Checks the time on his watch. It has gone midnight. He reaches for the telephone, taps out a number from memory. A woman's voice, surprised, answers.

DOMINIQUE
(*off*)

Hello?

KAROL

Dominique?

Karol speaks French fluently. Dominique is not sure who is calling.

DOMINIQUE
(*off*)

Yes . . .

168

KAROL

It's me, Karol. I'm calling from Warsaw . . .

Dominique does not answer.

From Poland.

Dominique still does not answer.

I'm sorry. I just wanted to hear your voice. Say something. Anything . . .

At that moment he hears the clatter of the receiver being replaced at the end of the line. He holds the receiver to his ear for a while longer and only puts it down when he hears the intermittent signal. He looks at the bust of the woman with sudden distaste. He get up from the bed and opens the door to the warehouse. He looks quite funny in his short briefs. He goes up to the switches and turns off the light. When he returns to the packing-room, the bust is in the darkness.

INT. WAREHOUSE. DAY

In the huge warehouse full of enormous containers Karol is giving instructions to his colleagues. He is walking along surrounded by a number of people. He points out two containers.

KAROL

Bananas?

A Colleague confirms.

Cold storage in Łódź. Their time'll come. They're too cheap at the moment.

He does not stop as he walks through the warehouse, deciding where the stored goods will go. A Young Employee slips him some papers to sign.

YOUNG EMPLOYEE

Electronic equipment. Thailand to Russia.

Karol glances at the papers and gives them back to her.

KAROL

We'll hold on to it. My expert says it's good stuff. We'll distribute in Poland.

They walk on. Suddenly Karol stops and listens.

There's a fax coming in, Jacek.

Karol takes a key out of his pocket and hands it to Jacek. Jacek runs to the small packing-room at the end of the hall where the fax is on. He returns with a roll of paper.

JACEK
(*reading*)
From your secretary. 'Mr Chairman. Everything is fine with the Swiss. But there is an unpleasant matter. The small computer from your office has gone missing. Henryka.'

Karol takes the fax from Jacek and runs his eyes over it.

KAROL
The Swiss? I doubt it. They've only recently stopped cutting hands off for stealing.

He takes the key from Jacek.

Let me take a nap for half an hour. I've had a terrible night.

Karol goes to the packing-room, opens the door with the key. He sits down on the bed, lost in thought. He takes out his comb and mirror and, all the while thinking over the problem which is troubling him, combs his hair. Absentmindedly, he cleans the comb of hair and suddenly reaches for the phone. He presses the button to increase the volume of conversation and one of the memory buttons. A woman's voice answers.

KAROL
Henryka, it's me. Is the driver there?

HENRYKA
(*off*)
Yes, boss.

KAROL
Put him on.

The entire conversation can be clearly heard in the packing-room. Footsteps of a man approaching the phone at the other end can also be heard. The man speaks.

DRIVER
(off)

Yes, boss.

KAROL

Bronek. Take out your car keys.

A clanging of keys can be heard.

Hand them to Henryka.

DRIVER
(off)

I've handed them over.

KAROL

Now tell her, so that I can hear: Henryka, please go down to the garage, open the boot of the car and, if you find anything there, please bring it up. And don't put the receiver down.

We hear the Driver follow the instructions. During this, his voice clearly changes. We hear a woman's footsteps leave the office.

KAROL

Are you there?

DRIVER
(off)

Yes, boss.

KAROL

Do something so that I can hear you all the time. Breathe loudly or sing.

DRIVER
(off)

I can't sing, boss. Only what I learnt when I was young . . .

KAROL

Sing.

The Driver obviously finds it hard to start. He sings quietly and weakly.

DRIVER
(*singing off*)
'To the barricades, you nation of workers, lift high the banners red . . .'

KAROL
Nice song.

DRIVER
(*singing off*)
La la la la la, la la la la la . . .

KAROL
Can't you remember the words?

DRIVER
(*off*)
No, I can't. Don't torture me, boss. I took it.

KAROL
Took what?

DRIVER
(*off*)
The computer. I thought it would get blamed on the Swiss.

We hear a woman's fast footsteps again. Henryka takes the receiver from the Driver.

HENRYKA
(*off*)
You certainly have your wits about you, boss. It was there.

KAROL
I know.

HENRYKA
(*off*)
He's crying here.

KAROL
What else can he do? I thought he was honest. He spent so many years in the public prosecutor's office . . . What's the world coming to, Henryka?

HENRYKA

True. Are we giving him the sack?

KAROL

On the contrary. We've got him eating out of our hands now.

Karol switches off, finishing the conversation. Happy with what has happened he lies down on the bed. For a long while, he looks at the alabaster bust. He presses a bell. Jacek's face appears at the door.

JACEK

Yes, boss?

KAROL

Bring me a box, Mr Jacek. And some tape.

JACEK

A big one?

KAROL

No. From bananas.

Jacek disappears and Karol looks at the bust with an unpleasant smile on his face. After a while, Jacek arrives with the box and some adhesive tape. Karol points to the bust.

KAROL

Wrap it up.

Jacek skilfully wraps the bust and sticks the box down with tape.

Hide it.

JACEK

Where?

KAROL

I don't know . . . The fridge.

Jacek leaves and Karol remains lying down for a while longer, his eyes open and a hard expression on his face. Then he shuts his eyes.

INT. NOTARY'S OFFICE. DAY

The notary's office is furnished with old, dilapidated furniture. The Notary, without much skill, just about manages to cope with the rickety

typewriter. Karol is dictating; he tries to match the rhythm of his words to the typewriting skills of the Notary.

KAROL
In the event of my death . . . my . . . death . . . all my . . . personal belongings . . . personal belongings . . . and property . . . as well as any sums of . . . sums of . . .

This time the Notary is ahead of Karol. He prompts.

NOTARY
Money.

KAROL
Money in my . . . bank . . . accounts . . . I leave . . .

He hesitates for a moment, not knowing how to phrase it.

I leave . . . to my ex- . . . ex-wife . . . Dominique.

The Notary, surprised, lifts his eyes from the keyboard. Karol, pretending not to understand the reason for his surprise, explains.

Dominique. Spelt with a 'q', 'u', 'e' at the end.

The Notary diligently taps out the letters clearly spelt out to him. The expression of doubt does not leave his face.

EXT. IN FRONT OF THE PALACE OF CULTURE. DAY

There is a good deal of space between the Marriott and the Palace of Culture. Traders from Russia have settled there. They are buying and selling everything. We see the silhouette of the Marriott. The Palace of Culture is surrounded by convenient walls – to lean against – which border the stairs. Karol is leaning against one of them. He stares into the distance, intensely preoccupied with his own thoughts. He does not notice Mikołaj approaching. Mikołaj leans against the other side of the wall, but even when he is so near, Karol does not notice him. Mikołaj smiles and moves towards Karol until he is directly opposite him. He waves his hand in front of Karol's eyes. Karol returns to reality. Mikołaj smiles.

> MIKOŁAJ
>
> Why did you drag me out here?

> KAROL
>
> I'm afraid the office may be bugged. There's so much equipment around . . .

> MIKOŁAJ
>
> By who?

Karol shrugs.

> KAROL
>
> Who knows. I wanted to tell you something.

> MIKOŁAJ
>
> Go ahead.

> KAROL
>
> Don't be surprised to see my obituaries in the papers. One of them's going to be signed by you.

> MIKOŁAJ
>
> Okay.

> KAROL
>
> It occurred to me a few days ago. I suddenly remembered our meeting on the rubbish dump . . .

MIKOŁAJ

Okay.

KAROL

That's not all. My lawyer's got my will . . .

From a large wallet with credit cards nestling in the various compartments, Karol pulls out a card with some writing on it and hands it to Mikołaj. Names, telephone numbers and addresses are noted there. Mikołaj glances, folds the card and hides it in his pocket.

You're my executor.

MIKOŁAJ

Do you want me to drag her from France?

Karol nods.

Will she come?

KAROL

It's a lot of money. She'll come.

They stay silent for a moment.

Don't you want to know what it's all about?

MIKOŁAJ

I think I know. You didn't ask any questions either.

Karol looks at Mikołaj with friendship.

KAROL

Thanks.

MIKOŁAJ

You'll need a passport again.

KAROL

Yes.

MIKOŁAJ

Polish?

KAROL

Yes, Polish. But with a good name. Bush, for example.

MIKOŁAJ

With an 'h'? It's going to cost you.

KAROL

You can make it with a 'ch'. I've left you my address on the card
there. There's no telephone. Send the driver if you need to.

MIKOŁAJ

Bronek? He'll open his big mouth.

KAROL

No . . . Mikołaj?

Mikołaj turns to face him. They are now looking into each other's eyes.

Will you do something for me even if you don't understand
why? And you don't like it?

MIKOŁAJ

Foul play? Grassing?

KAROL

You could put it that way . . .

Mikołaj nods.

Don't worry. I'm not getting you mixed up in anything.

MIKOŁAJ
(*solemnly*)

I know.

INT. REGISTRY OFFICE. DAY

*A woman's hand tears Karol's photograph from his identity card. An
unpleasant crackling of paper. The same hand feeds the photograph and
identity card into a shredder. Several turnings of the knives and narrow
strips of paper from what remains of the card and photograph fall into
the waste-paper bin. The hand stamps a document which is lying on the
desk, signs it and hands it to Bronek.*

REGISTRY CLERK

My condolences.

Bronek thanks her with a solemn nod. He leaves.

EXT. STREET IN FRONT OF THE OFFICE. DAY

Bronek leaves the office and gets into the car. He turns to the back seat and hands the document he has just received to Karol who is sitting there. Karol reads and points out to Bronek.

> KAROL
>
> Do you know what's next?

He taps the document with his finger. Bronek looks at him in disbelief.

> BRONEK
>
> What?

> KAROL
>
> We need someone to bury, Bronek.

> BRONEK
>
> A corpse?

Karol nods. Bronek swallows hard.

> You're not thinking of . . .

He runs a finger across his throat in an unequivocal gesture. Karol grimaces with distaste.

> Well . . . we'll just have to buy one then. You can buy anything these days.

> KAROL
>
> You think so?

> BRONEK
>
> They trade in anything.

He looks closely at Karol.

> He should be your size.

He thinks it over a moment, then brightens up.

> You wouldn't mind an import, would you, boss? From the east?

KAROL
An Arab?

Bronek makes a nondescript movement with his hand.

BRONEK
No, nearer home. There's a huge market. It'd be easiest.
You've no idea what goes on there.

KAROL
Good thinking.

BRONEK
Thank you, boss.

He looks at his watch.

You've got an appointment at the funeral parlour.

*Karol nods. The car moves away from in front of the office and
disappears down the street.*

INT. FUNERAL PARLOUR. DAY

*The funeral parlour is decorated in black with silver ornaments. The
middle-aged Woman is polite, subdued in the face of death.*

WOMAN
Could I ask you for the death certificate, please?

*Karol opens his leather briefcase and takes out the document already
known to us. The Woman notes the details in her book.*

May I take a photocopy, please?

*Karol nods. The Woman gets up and, with dignity, arranges the
document on the photocopier. She understands what it is like to lose
someone dear to you.*

Can we discuss the details of the funeral?

Karol adapts his manner to the atmosphere.

KAROL
Don't worry about the cost. Go by your experience. It should
look decent.

WOMAN

I understand. Just so I've got something to go by . . . We've got Polish and American cars for transporting the coffin. An American car costs one and a half million.

KAROL

A month's salary. Fine, I'll take an American one.

WOMAN

I understand. There's still the matter of what to put on the headstone. I take it it's to be in marble?

KAROL

Yes. As simple as possible. 'Karol Karol 1957–1992'.

INT. POWĄZKOWSKI CEMETERY CHURCH. DAY

The Organist studies the notes which Karol has obviously given him. He has spread them out on the organ keyboard. He sings to himself, turns to Karol.

ORGANIST

It's beautiful. What is it?

KAROL

Van den Budenmayer. Dutch.

The Organist plays quietly to himself. The organ sounds grand and sad in the empty church. Hearing footsteps on the stairs, Karol turns. Looking around and smiling, Bronek enters with a newspaper – open on the obituaries page – in his hand. Karol reads in silence.

'. . . a man whom we all loved.' Signed, Employees. Very good . . .

Bronek chuckles as he takes back the paper.

BRONEK

I've just bought it. Phoned the office. Henryka's in tears.

He cannot stop himself from laughing. Only after a while does he manage to quieten down and listen.

Beautiful music.

Karol nods.

> I can't wait for you, boss. I've got an important appointment
> at the airport.

KAROL

> You go on, Bronek. I'll listen for a bit.

*Bronek goes down while Karol continues listening to the quiet organ
music for a while longer.*

EXT. IN FRONT OF THE WAREHOUSE. DUSK

*A large refrigerated lorry drives away from the huge warehouse. The
characteristic lettering of an eastern transport company can be read on
the side of the container.*

INT. WAREHOUSE. NIGHT

*In the enormous warehouse full of containers which we already know,
Karol and Bronek are leaning over something. Karol grimaces.*

BRONEK

> Couldn't be better, boss. It's impossible to identify.

KAROL

> But what happened to him?

BRONEK

> His head got crushed. Leaned out of the tram window a bit
> too far.

*Karol takes two steps back. He lifts the coffin lid. Bronek helps. They
arrange the lid on the oak coffin.*

KAROL

> I'll manage.

*Bronek bows and leaves. Karol remains alone in the empty warehouse.
He waits a moment longer until he hears the door close behind Bronek,
then takes out the two-franc coin from his pocket. He turns it around in
his fingers for a while, lifts the coffin lid and throws the coin in. Then he
carefully nails the coffin down with a large hammer. At the first few
hollow blows, he hears a distinct rustling. He stops, looks up. Dozens of*

frightened pigeons are flying around under the warehouse roof. Karol watches them, hammer in hand. The pigeons calm down after a while – this obviously pleases Karol. Trying to make as little noise as possible, he hammers more nails into the coffin. He uses the side of the hammer. The nails slide in smoothly and the banging is far quieter than before.

EXT. POWĄZKOWSKI CEMETERY. DAY

Among thick tree trunks and old tombstones, the coffin, expertly suspended on ropes, slowly descends into the gaping hole. This is the old, beautiful part of the Powązkowski Cemetery. An orchestra is playing Van den Budenmayer. Several dozen people have turned up at the funeral. We easily recognize Jurek, Mikołaj, who is standing next to a woman in a black coat, Bronek, the Owner of the foreign exchange kiosk, the Blonde, the Tall Man, several workers from the enormous warehouse, Jadwiga and a few other of Karol's clients. Karol, himself, we only catch sight of after a while. He has hidden himself behind a thick tree, thirty, forty, fifty yards away from the grave into which the undertakers are now lowering the coffin with his body. Karol takes out from behind the tree, raises a pair of binoculars to his eyes. He focuses them on the woman in the black coat standing next to Mikołaj. Now we

*can recognize her – it is Dominique. She watches the ceremony for a
while, then makes a strange, vague gesture near her face. Karol watches
carefully. He sees that Dominique is wiping tears away. She remains
alone when everybody else leaves the graveside. Mikołaj waits for her
discreetly a few paces away. Dominique is crying. Karol takes the
binoculars away from his eyes. He is touched – he, too, has tears in his
eyes. He watches her small, slim silhouette standing alone over the fresh
grave. Behaving discreetly, he leaves in the direction of the cemetery
exit.*

INT. HOTEL APARTMENT. NIGHT

*Black screen. We hear a key grating. The door opens, Dominique's
silhouette enters, the door closes and, for a moment again, the screen is
black. The sound of a light being switched on, and the room is lit.
Dominique has entered the apartment and now stands, shattered,
leaning against the wall. She removes her coat, which slides down the
wall and falls to the floor. She takes a few steps further into the room.
She notices an alabaster bust of a woman standing on the dressing-table.
She is not sure whether it was there when she moved into the apartment.
She is drawn by the woman's delicate face. She approaches it and
touches the nose, lips, eyes. For some obscure reason, the atmosphere
from the funeral returns. Automatically, without thinking, she undoes
her skirt and, not caring that it's slipping down, enters the bedroom.
Again, for a moment, there is complete darkness. Dominique switches on
the light and, with a muted cry of fear, steps back. In bed, undressed
and half-covered with a sheet, lies Karol. Dominique, dumbstruck,
makes as if to run away, but all she can do is pull up her skirt, which
slips down again anyway.*

DOMINIQUE

Karol . . .

Karol answers in French.

KAROL

Yes. I wanted you to come. I wanted to be sure. And I didn't
want to have to ask any more.

Dominique is in no state to say anything except repeat his name.

183

                    DOMINIQUE
  Karol.

*Karol, as he once did in Paris, in the hairdressing salon, holds out his
hand to her.*

                    KAROL
  You cried at the cemetery . . . Why?

*Dominique nods, touched. Tears appear in her eyes again. She answers
quietly.*

                    DOMINIQUE
  Because you were dead.

                    KAROL
  Can I touch your hand?

*Dominique takes a step in the direction of the bed and Karol, very
carefully, touches her hand. Gently, he draws her to him.*

  Sit down.

Dominique obediently sits down on the bed.

  Can I lay my head here?

*Without saying anything, Dominique moves closer and Karol lays his
head on her thighs. For a moment, Dominique holds her hands over his
head, then, slowly, lowers them and touches his hair. She starts stroking
it gently.*

                    (softly)
  I've wanted to lay my head here for such a long time . . .

*Dominique leans over his face, turns it towards her. She now sees it close
to her, leans down a bit more and lightly kisses his lips, still reasonably
apprehensive that Karol might disappear just as he had appeared.
Karol equally lightly touches her lips with his. He lifts his arms and
plaits some of Dominique's cascading hair into a braid. Their lips meet
with increasing intensity and strength. The love scene slowly turns erotic.
There is more desire, more tension in the kisses, the breathing becomes
heavier. Karol reaches for the switch and turns off the light.*

INT. HOTEL RECEPTION. NIGHT

Bronek leans over the reception counter with a smile.

> **BRONEK**
> Ewa . . . I'm here according to our agreement.

Ewa looks at him surprised. She is tired and half asleep.

> It's me, Ewa. Passport from apartment 1423. I'll bring it back
> shortly.

*It all comes back to Ewa. She reaches towards the pigeonholes and takes
the passport. She places it on the counter. With the same smile as at the
beginning, Bronek covers it with his hand.*

INT. HOTEL APARTMENT. NIGHT

We hear Dominique's voice in the darkness.

> **DOMINIQUE**
> I want to see you . . .

She turns on the light. They are in a different position now. Karol's face is leaning over Dominique's. We clearly sense that they are beginning to make love and that both of them experience it as something wonderful. Karol switches off the light for a second time. It is dark.

DISSOLVE TO:

EXT. CHIMNEY. SPECIAL EFFECTS. DAY

We hear Karol's and Dominique's breathing getting heavier and heavier.

A different, deeper blackness with a tiny point of light. The camera moves and, slowly at first, then with increasing speed, draws closer to the point of light. The effect should be similar to that achieved by placing the camera at the bottom of a very deep chimney and tracking upwards. The light gets nearer, fills a fifth of the screen, then a third, then half and, suddenly, the camera, as if freed, emerges from the blackness into bright, blinding light. It stays in the brightness for a while.

FADE TO:

INT. HOTEL APARTMENT. NIGHT/DAY

Karol's and Dominique's faces appear lying next to each other. They are both still breathing heavily, having only just finished making love. Their heavy breathing grows quiet. Silence.

KAROL
You moaned louder than on the phone . . .

DOMINIQUE
Yes . . .

Karol opens his eyes. He looks at her for a while, then closes his eyes again. Dominique smiles faintly. Karol stretches out his hand and touches her face as if wanting to remember its shape.

I never thought you looked like this. Are you tired?

Karol nods without opening his eyes. Dominique parts his hands, draws him closer and rests her head on his chest.

May I sleep like this?

Karol nods. Dominique closes her eyes, falls asleep. Karol does not sleep. After a long while, he opens his eyes and, seeing that Dominique has fallen asleep, looks ahead into the distance.

At dawn, Dominique, cuddled up to a pillow as she had fallen asleep cuddled up to Karol, stirs. Karol, who is knotting his tie, freezes for a moment but, seeing that Dominique is still asleep, puts on his jacket, glancing twice at his watch. Quietly, so as not to wake the sleeping Dominique, he walks up to the window. Below, he sees a Florist arranging her wares. He smiles, for a while gazes affectionately at Dominique's hair spread out over the pillow, leans over, holds out his hand as if wanting to stroke the hair, restrains himself, gets up and, gently pulling the door to, leaves the room.

EXT. IN FRONT OF THE HOTEL. DAY

Karol approaches the Florist. He pulls out a wad of notes from his back pocket and gathers up the enormous bouquet which the Florist had prepared for the whole day. Laden down with the bouquet, he returns to the hotel. On the way, he turns into a travel agency.

INT. HOTEL APARTMENT. DAY

Dominique is woken by a quiet cracking sound. She opens her eyes, calm, dreamy, a smile on her face. Only after a while does unease creep in.

> DOMINIQUE
> Karol . . .

Nobody, of course, answers. Dominique jumps up from the bed, wraps a sheet around herself and runs into the living-room.

> Karol!

With fading hope, she opens the bathroom door, turns on the light. Obviously, Karol is not there either. Dominique runs up to the telephone and immediately puts it down again, because there is nobody she can call. She sits down on the bed and repeats pitifully.

> Karol . . .

She picks up the receiver again. She finds a business card in her handbag and calls.

HENRYKA
(off)

MiKa Company. Can I help you?

DOMINIQUE

May I speak to Mikołaj, please? It's Dominique.

HENRYKA
(off)

I'll just put you through to the chairman.

MIKOŁAJ
(off)

Hello . . .

DOMINIQUE

It's Dominique. Where's Karol?

MIKOŁAJ
(off)

He's dead.

His French is not bad.

DOMINIQUE

He is not dead. I saw him last night . . .

MIKOŁAJ
(off)

You were at his funeral yesterday.

DOMINIQUE

I was not at his funeral! He's alive!

MIKOŁAJ
(off)

I'm sorry.

DOMINIQUE

Help me to find him, Mikołaj. I love him.

MIKOŁAJ
(off)

Right. Section 23, tomb number 2675, and the cemetery's
called Powązkowski in Polish. Po . . . wąz . . . kow . . . ski.

Dominique hears a knock on the door. She brightens up.

DOMINIQUE
He's back. He's here. Sorry, I've got to hang up.

MIKOŁAJ
(off)
I kind of doubt it.

Dominique does not listen to the last sentence. She replaces the receiver and runs to the door. She opens it. Two strangers stand in the doorway. Behind them, several armed policemen.

INSPECTOR
Dominique Insdorf?

DOMINIQUE
Yes . . .

The men enter. Dominique, wrapped in her sheet, retreats a step.

INT. TRAVEL AGENCY. DAY

Karol opens the door, just about managing with the bouquet. He approaches a pleasant Stewardess. He puts the bouquet aside on the counter, takes out his wallet and from the wallet pulls out an airplane ticket.

KAROL
I'm supposed to be flying out to Hong Kong today. At eleven-thirty. I'd like to cancel.

STEWARDESS
It's a bit late.

Karol looks at his watch.

KAROL
It's still nearly two hours before the flight. I've got a right . . .

The Stewardess smiles pleasantly.

STEWARDESS
You forgot to put your watch forward. The clocks went forward last night. There won't be any problem though.

There are a lot of volunteers for that flight. May I see your
ticket please . . .

*Karol turns pale when he hears about the change of time. He looks at
his watch and compares it to the time on the electronic clock above the
counter.*

KAROL

What time is it?

STEWARDESS

Ten-thirty.

Karol automatically hands the ticket to the Stewardess.

KAROL

Can I make a call?

*Without waiting for an answer he pulls the phone from in front of the
Stewardess. He dials quickly. Henryka answers.*

HENRYKA
(*off*)

MiKa Company. Can I help you?

KAROL

It's Karol here, Henryka. Get me Mikołaj right away.

First silence, then Henryka's cry of horror.

HENRYKA
(*off*)

Aaaaaa . . . Aaaaaaaaaa . . .

*She puts the phone down. Karol immediately dials again. He shouts
down the receiver.*

KAROL

It's me, Henryka, it's me! Please . . .

HENRYKA
(*off*)

Please don't do such things . . . Ohhhhhhhh . . .

*We hear a crash on the other end of the line as if someone has collapsed
by the phone.*

KAROL
(*shouting*)

Hello! Hello!

INT. HOTEL APARTMENT. DAY

*Dominique has got dressed. She comes out of the bedroom. Three men
are waiting in the living-room.*

INSPECTOR
Your passport, please.

*The Interpreter translates impassively. He is elderly and balding.
Dominique reaches into her handbag and remembers.*

DOMINIQUE
It's at the front desk.

INSPECTOR
Then call downstairs.

*Dominique calls and asks for her passport to be brought up. She turns to
the Inspector – something has just occurred to her.*

DOMINIQUE
I'm a French citizen.

INSPECTOR
We know. The Consulate's already been informed.
Someone's coming. You have the right to remain silent until
he comes . . .

The Interpreter translates without interest.

DOMINIQUE
I've got nothing to hide. I'd just like to know what all this is
about.

INSPECTOR
You've already begun executing the will, haven't you? You've
got a meeting with . . .

DOMINIQUE
Yes.

INSPECTOR

He was a very rich man, your ex-husband, wasn't he?

Dominique loses her self-confidence.

DOMINIQUE

Yeeees . . .

At that moment, the door opens and the Bellboy enters. Dominique holds out her hand, the Bellboy gives her her passport. Dominique checks whether the passport is hers. Everything is in order.

Thank you.

The Interpreter translates. The Bellboy is obviously waiting for the tip to materialize.

INSPECTOR

That'll be all, thank you.

He gives him such a look that the Bellboy quickly leaves the room. The Inspector holds out his hand and Dominique gives him the passport.

INT. HOTEL LIFT AND CORRIDOR. DAY

Karol, agitated, with the huge bouquet still in his arms, goes up in the lift. He gets out at his floor, passes the Bellboy going the other way and, immediately around the corner outside the door to Dominique's apartment, comes across several armed Police and Plainclothes Policemen. Seeing them, Karol retreats. One of the Policemen stops him.

POLICEMAN

Stop!

Karol stops and swallows hard. The Policeman walks up to him.

And who have you come to see?

KAROL

Wrong floor. I've got some flowers for room 1243.

The Policeman parts the flowers, checking to see if anything else is lurking in the bouquet.

POLICEMAN

Your name?

KAROL

Karol Busch.

POLICEMAN

ID, please.

Karol pulls out a passport from his enormous wallet. The Policeman gives it back to him with a smile.

Not a bad name. I wouldn't hang around here if I were you.

INT. HOTEL APARTMENT. DAY

The Inspector examines the passport, flicks through the pages.

INSPECTOR

We don't believe your ex-husband died a natural death.

DOMINIQUE

What?

INSPECTOR

We have proof that you were here the day he died. The stamp is in your passport. Why?

The Inspector shows Dominique the stamp on an open page of her passport. The Interpreter continues without the slightest emotion.

DOMINIQUE

He's not dead. He's alive!

INSPECTOR

Who?

DOMINIQUE

Karol! My husband!

INSPECTOR

So whose funeral were you at yesterday at eleven-thirty?

Dominique does not say anything for a while, then sits down heavily on the chair. She answers quietly.

DOMINIQUE

His.

INSPECTOR

Then who's alive?

Dominique hides her face in her hands. She shakes her head.

DOMINIQUE

No one . . .

In the doorway, out of breath, stands the short Consulate Representative. He approaches and greets Dominique. He shakes hands with the Inspector – it looks as if they know each other. The Inspector gently explains.

INSPECTOR

We're going to have to detain you. Please don't worry, everything will be meticulously looked into. We expect an exhumation tomorrow.

The Representative waves his hand in resignation. Dominique raises her eyes.

EXT. IN FRONT OF THE HOTEL. DAY

Karol dashes out of the hotel. He throws the bouquet, which is getting in his way, into a bin as he passes and misses. He looks around in desperation. He notices a blue Volkswagen stopping. He runs up to the car. The Blonde's window is open, she is parking.

KAROL

Do me a favour. I'm in a terrible hurry. Can you give me a lift to the Marriott.

The Blonde smiles at him and without saying a word bends her arm at the elbow in an unequivocal gesture. The smile disappears from her face.

Please!

The Blonde slowly winds her window up, catching Karol's finger. He pulls it from the trap at the last moment. He runs off, sucking his finger and waving to a passing taxi which goes by without paying him any attention.

EXT. PIŁSUDSKI SQUARE. DAY

Karol runs for all he's worth across the huge, empty square.

INT. OFFICE IN THE MARRIOTT HOTEL. DAY

*Karol bursts through his office door and on seeing Henryka puts a finger
to his lips. Henryka backs away into her armchair. She grabs the
armrests to stop herself from screaming. Karol runs up to her – she is
more and more terrified – and grabs her by the hand.*

> KAROL
> It's me, Henryka. It's me.

*Without waiting for her to calm down, he runs to the office door and
bursts in. Mikołaj is pacing up and down the room.*

> MIKOŁAJ
> What're you doing here? You shouldn't . . .

> KAROL
> Call it all off. Put it straight. All of it.

> MIKOŁAJ
> How?

Karol calms down. He does not know the answer to Mikołaj's question.

> What's happened?

> KAROL
> I didn't know they put the clocks forward last night. I thought
> it had just gone nine but it had gone ten. I called you.
> Henryka fainted . . .

*Saying this, he realizes what nonsense it all is. He sits down heavily in
the chair.*

> MIKOŁAJ
> I called the police at ten, as you wanted.

> KAROL
> I know. Mikołaj . . . I love her.

*Karol raises his eyes and looks at Mikołaj, who is moved by his
confession,*

MIKOŁAJ
(*seriously*)

She loves you, too.

Karol grabs his head. He groans quietly. After a long while, he suddenly regains his energy.

KAROL

I'll turn myself in. I'll tell them everything. I'll do time, I don't care . . .

MIKOŁAJ

You'll give me away, too, not to mention Bronek. Go ahead, you're right.

Karol hides his face in his hands again. He groans louder now.

INT. HAIRDRESSING SALON. DAY

Jurek peers into the depths of the oven with great concentration. This lasts a fair while.

JUREK

It's ready.

He opens the oven and takes out a beautifully baked pie. He is wearing an apron and, with pleasure and skill, takes out the pie. He cuts it carefully with a knife and suddenly starts giggling. Only now do we see that Karol is in the kitchen, too. He watches with apprehension.

KAROL

What is it?

JUREK

Nothing. I just remembered identifying you after the exhumation. We recognized you. Mikołaj puked . . .

Karol does not have much of a sense of humour on the subject. Jurek wraps the pie in clean paper and pours some fruit salad into a jar.

I've made some fruit salad, too. Cherries. Karol . . . how about snails some day? We've got them in our garden. I could make a stew . . .

KAROL

Has the lawyer been?

JUREK

He came by. Charges enough . . .

Karol waves the thought away – it is not important.

He said . . .

KAROL

What?

Jurek packs the pie and fruit salad into a plastic bag.

JUREK

That he sees a little light at the end of the tunnel.

EXT. OUTSIDE THE HAIRDRESSING SALON. DUSK

Karol, carrying the plastic bag, comes out of the hairdressing salon, passes by the dull, dusty display window. There are several mannequin heads in the window advertising wigs which are obviously made in the salon. One of these heads is a white alabaster bust of a woman. It is not in the best condition – covered in dead flies and dust, a wig perched askew on its head. For a moment, we stop at the image of the bust.

EXT. PRISON WALL. DUSK

Karol, with the plastic bag, walks alongside the very long prison wall.

INT. PRISON DUTY-ROOM. DUSK

Karol passes the bag through the window. The Guard takes it and looks questioningly at Karol. Karol takes something quite small from his pocket and passes it to the Guard as if he were going to shake his hand.

KAROL

May I take a look today?

The Guard nods in agreement. Karol approaches the bars, the Guard opens the gate with a great clatter and with an even greater clatter closes it behind him. Karol shudders at the noise.

You'll let her know I'm here.

The Guard nods again. He opens the prison courtyard gate for Karol.

EXT. PRISON COURTYARD. DUSK

Karol turns his gaze up to the barred window. The light is on just as it is in all the other windows. Karol pulls out a pair of small, theatre binoculars and focuses. He now sees the window much closer. He waits. After a moment, in the window – obviously built in such a way that no one can get near to it – a shadow appears as if someone were waving their hand. Karol watches the moving shadow with tears in his eyes.

FADE OUT.

Against this background – END CREDITS.

Three Colours: Red

CREDITS

CAST

VALENTINE   Irène Jacob
JUDGE   Jean-Louis Tritignant

CREW

Director   Krzysztof Kieślowski
Screenplay   Krzysztof Kieślowski,
     Krzysztof Piesiewicz
Cinematography   Piotr Sobociński
Editor   Jacques Witta
Art Director   Claude Lenoir
Music   Zbigniew Preisner
Sound   Jean-Claude Laureaux
Sound Mixer   William Flageollet
Executive Producer   Yvon Crenn
Producer   Marin Karmitz
Production Companies   Tor Productions/MK2 Productions
     SA/CED Productions/France 3
     Cinema/CAB Productions

INT. MICHEL'S FLAT. DAY

A finger taps out twelve numbers on a telephone keyboard. The camera pans quickly along the telephone cable following the tone running through it.

INT./EXT. TELEPHONE EXCHANGE. SPECIAL EFFECTS. DAY

We hear a connection being made. The camera speeds in fast moves along endlessly long, intricately criss-crossing telephone cables, through a telephone exchange, electronic links. Bulbs light up, flaps jump into place, lights flash. We hear an increasing number – dozens – of mixed telephone conversations in various languages; we cannot make out a single word. The camera, following thick cables on the ground (it is raining), immerses itself into the sea. Increasing noise of connections and conversations. Hell. The camera emerges from the sea – the sun is shining – and descends into a tunnel full of thick cables, connections; lights flash in the telephone exchange. Suddenly the camera comes to a standstill.

Against this background: TITLE CREDITS.

We hear an engaged tone. The camera moves back with enormous speed. It flies past coils of cables, the exchange, connections and, with the engaged tone, returns to the telephone where the number was being dialled at the beginning of the scene.

INT. MICHEL'S FLAT. DAY

A man's hand replaces the receiver and picks it up again. A finger taps out the first number.

INT. AUGUST'S FLAT. DAY

August, in his thirties, is already in his coat. On the table, the remains of breakfast. He quickly searches for some books, packs them. There are several of them. He finds one near the unmade bed. He picks up the last

*of the books from a shelf. He slips an elastic band around them, briefly
checks its strength and places the pile of books on the table. He checks
how many cigarettes are left in the packet before putting it in his pocket.
He finds a long, bright-red leash and attaches it to the collar of a
medium-sized, black, shaggy dog which is overjoyed at the prospect of
going for a walk. They leave the flat.*

INT. AUGUST'S STAIRWELL. DAY

*August runs down the stairs, automatically checking to see if there are
any letters in his postbox. The dog tugs at its leash. August opens the
stairwell door. They step outside.*

INT. STREET OUTSIDE AUGUST'S FLAT. DAY

*August, with the dog on its red leash, runs across to the other side of
the street. It is sunny, puddles glisten after the recent rain. The dog
wants to get to the small square as quickly as possible. As they pass one
of the buildings on the opposite side of the street, the camera leaves
them and stops at that building. We hear a telephone ringing. The
camera tracks upwards, stops briefly at a public telephone, slowly leads
us to a window on the third floor and tracks inside. The ringing gets
louder and louder.*

INT. VALENTINE'S FLAT. DAY

*The camera tracks into Valentine's flat and, following the sound of the
ringing, comes to the telephone. After the sixth ring, the answering
machine switches on.*

> VALENTINE
> (*off*)
> Hello, this is Valentine. Please leave a message after the tone.

We hear the tone and a man's voice.

> MICHEL
> (*off*)
> Valentine . . . Valentine, are you there? Valentine!

*Just when we think there is nobody at home, Valentine's smiling face
appears at the telephone. She lifts the receiver while eating yogurt with*

pieces of banana in it from a plastic pot. We briefly catch sight of a
picture of two red cherries on the pot.

> VALENTINE
>
> I'm here, Michel. I was just having breakfast.

She swallows the yogurt.

> MICHEL
> *(off)*
>
> It was engaged a moment ago. Now the answering machine's
> on. Are you alone?

> VALENTINE
>
> Yes.

> MICHEL
> *(off)*
>
> Completely?

> VALENTINE
>
> Completely. It was engaged because the agency called. We
> were arranging a photo session. When did you get back?

> MICHEL
> *(off)*
>
> Yesterday. I phoned but you weren't in. Our car was stolen.
> In Poland. Everything. Passports, money . . .

> VALENTINE
>
> What happened?

> MICHEL
> *(off)*
>
> Some nice guy put us up in his office. There are some good
> people there . . .

> VALENTINE
>
> Michel . . . I did a stupid thing last night.

Michel's voice is clearly uneasy.

> MICHEL
> *(off)*
>
> What?

VALENTINE

I slept with your jacket all night long. I wanted to be with you.

MICHEL
(*off*)

Valentine, I can't now.

VALENTINE

I know.

She pulls out a man's red jacket from her unmade bed. With the cordless phone in her hand and glancing at her watch, Valentine is getting ready to go out. She finds her handbag, throws in all the bits and pieces she needs for the day, finds her scarf behind a chair.

VALENTINE

What's the weather like over there?

MICHEL
(*off*)

Pouring, as usual.

Valentine looks towards the window. Patches of sunlight on the floorboards. The camera tracks to the window. On the other side of the street, August, not clearly recognizable, is returning home with his dog. He passes through his gate.

VALENTINE
(*off*)

It's sunny here. Already warm.

MICHEL
(*off*)

What were you doing last night? When I called?

VALENTINE
(*off*)

I went to the cinema.

MICHEL
(*off*)

I'll call tomorrow. Maybe you'll be in?

Valentine steps into frame, closes the window.

I'll be in.

She replaces the receiver, then pulls one arm through the sleeve of her coat and, without too much effort, covers the bed with a blanket. It is clear that she is not very organized. She throws a few coloured pillows on the bed.

EXT. IN FRONT OF AUGUST'S AND VALENTINE'S FLATS. DAY

August, with his pile of books held together by the elastic band, runs out of the gate and gets into his jeep. The car moves off and, making use of the purpose-built track across the centre stretch of grass, makes a U-turn on the two-way street, passes the public call-box and, after a few yards, brakes. He reverses and stops by the call-box. With the engine still running, August gets out and enters the call-box. He inserts a coin, taps out a number. A woman, Karin, answers.

KARIN
(*off*)
Good morning. Detailed weather report.

August gently replaces the receiver, smiles. Everything is all right. He does not notice the coin fall on the floor, rejected by the telephone. He gets into his car and moves off. At that same time, the gate of the building next to the call-box opens and Valentine, already in her coat, emerges. She takes a few steps and disappears into the doorway of a small café – Joseph's.

INT. CAFÉ. DAY

Valentine, as she does no doubt every day, goes up to the one-armed bandit, inserts a coin and forcefully pulls the lever. Coloured lemons, cherries and apples flash in the little display window and the machine stops at two pictures of a cherry with the wording 'BAR' in between. The machine groans. Valentine has lost and smiles, pleased. The Barman looks in her direction and gives her an 'okay' thumbs-up sign.

BARMAN
Lose?

Valentine smiles broadly, nods. She copies the Barman's thumbs-up. She places another coin, which she had obviously got ready beforehand – for the newspaper – on the bar counter. Pleased, she leaves the café.

EXT. IN FRONT OF VALENTINE'S FLAT. DAY

A newspaper stand in front of the café. Valentine picks up the daily she has already paid for and, glancing through it, approaches a small car parked in front of her building. Her nose buried in the paper, she opens the door. She gets in, closes the door.

INT. PHOTOGRAPHIC STUDIO. DAY

Valentine, laughing, is chewing bubblegum. It looks a little as if she is doing it for show. And so she is. A Photographer, continuously clicking his camera, is circling around her in a studio. Valentine blows a bubble.

PHOTOGRAPHER
Blow harder, harder . . .

The bubble gets bigger and bigger.

Bigger. And tilt your head to the side. A bit more.

Valentine does as she is told, tries to be funny. She pouts, lifting her face; she tries to do the same, lowering her face; she shows her profile. The camera works quickly. The bubble bursts. With a sense of regret, Valentine licks what is left of the gum from her lips. The Photographer lowers his camera and comes closer.

What're you doing tonight?

VALENTINE
Trying to sleep.

PHOTOGRAPHER
Alone?

Valentine nods. She smiles apologetically.

Stop . . . Hold it.

For a moment, Valentine freezes the grimace on her lips, with her tongue sticking out. The Photographer quickly takes a dozen shots of the pose. The film's snapped. The Photographer disappears into the

darkroom, dimming the light. Valentine is left alone. She licks the rest of the gum from her lips. Angrily, she presses the ball of gum on to the table. She calls to the Photographer who is shut up in his darkroom.

VALENTINE
Don't come out. I'm getting changed.

She pulls at the buttons of her blouse.

INT. BALLET STUDIO. DAY

In the ballet studio, a dozen or so girls wearing thick, colourful leg-warmers are holding on to the bar, performing simple exercises. One leg held high in the air, then the other leg. This has been going on for some time and they are tired and sweaty. The Teacher, dressed like them, accentuates the rhythm of the music by tapping her cane on the floorboards. The dry cracks mingle with her high-pitched shouts.

TEACHER
And o-o-one and t-w-o-o-o and o-o-one . . .

Valentine wipes the sweat off her face. Following the Teacher's instructions, she takes a few steps on tiptoe further into the studio, then – like all the other girls – returns and again lifts a leg, clad in a red leg-warmer, and holds it a moment outstretched. A spasm of pain on her face. With her mouth open, she gasps for air. The leg is lifted again, held, then the other leg. Valentine is doing her best.

EXT. IN FRONT OF A GROCER'S SHOP. DAY

On the street Valentine greedily gulps down half a bottle of mineral water. Her throat moves to the rhythm of her large gulps. Drops of water trickle down her chin. It seems impossible, but nearly a litre of water disappears before our eyes without the bottle leaving Valentine's lips. August's jeep passes by just behind her. For a moment we recognize his face behind the steering wheel. Valentine does not pay any attention to it – it is only one of many cars passing (among them an old, brown Mercedes) – but the camera briefly picks it out from among the others. Valentine closes the bottle and hides what is left of the water in the large bag slung over her shoulder. A newspaper is sticking out of the bag. She calls into the shop.

VALENTINE
Have a good day!

She smiles, runs up to her car and gets in.

INT. HOTEL RECEPTION ROOM. NIGHT

A catwalk show of a prestigious fashion house is taking place in an elegant hotel. There are a dozen or so models behind the scenes in great confusion. Valentine straightens her short, colourful dress. The change of clothes is very fast. She stretches out her arm, someone hands her a fur coat, but, at the last moment, she pulls the arm from the sleeve and runs a few steps.

VALENTINE
Careful!

An electrician is swaying on a long ladder. Valentine catches hold of it just before it falls. Music begins to play. Valentine lets go of the now stable ladder, pulls the fur coat on at a run, and joins her colleagues stepping out on to the catwalk. They are all giggling because one of the models pulls an ugly face and drags her leg but, on stepping into the spotlights, she smiles radiantly, straightens herself and, in harmony with the music, dances energetically like all the other models, modelling yet another collection. Applause. Valentine moves well, lightly, flowingly. Returning after a few turns, she trips lightly over a step. She smiles to herself, easily regains her balance. They all return together and immediately, still on the run, take off furs, throw off shoes and stretch their arms out for the next piece of clothing.

EXT. CITY STREET. DUSK

Valentine gets into her car. It is already dusk. She switches on the radio, leans her head on the headrest and, for a moment, breathes with relief, rests. She straightens her hands, exercises her wrists and eyelids, opening and shutting her eyes. She starts the engine, regains her usual energy, moves off. After a few yards, she stops at some red lights. She does not notice August walking on the same side of the street, with his books fastened with elastic, and approaching the same set of lights. Valentine impatiently waits for the lights to change and when they do, she moves off, overtaking a cyclist who is starting clumsily. August wants to take advantage of the same green lights which Valentine crossed, so he takes a run and, at that moment, the elastic band holding his books together snaps. The books scatter all over the pavement and into the road. August bends over and gathers them. The gust of air created by passing cars blows the pages open. August bends down further. He reads the caption under the photograph on a page that is lying open randomly. He smiles as if he had just found what he had been looking for. He squats among his scattered books and, after flicking through a few pages, goes back to the one opened by the gust of air.

Valentine is driving fast, tapping her finger against the steering wheel in time to the music on the radio. She is now in a different part of town, outside the city centre. There is obviously some interference on the radio, the music disappears and we hear whistling. Valentine wants to retune it, but suddenly there is a loud, dull thud. She jams on the brakes, stops the car and turns around. She reverses and, in the headlights, sees a dog lying in a pool of blood. Valentine gets out, runs up to it, squats down. The large Alsatian is looking at her with tearful eyes. It whines quietly. Valentine looks about her helplessly – the street is empty. She tries to lift the dog. It is heavy. With great effort, Valentine drags it towards her car. She opens the back door and, helping herself with her knee, arranges the dog on the back seat. Her hands are covered in blood, she breathes heavily. She strokes the dog's head. It closes its eyes, surrendering to the caress. While she is stroking, Valentine discovers a collar around the dog's neck. There is a metal tab attached to it with the owner's address and the dog's name.

VALENTINE

Rita . . . Rita.

The dog opens her eyes. Valentine switches the light on in her car and finds a map of the city. The street where the dog's owner lives is outside of town, in a neighbourhood of villas. Valentine turns around, sees the dog's eyes gazing at her.

EXT. NEIGHBOURHOOD OF VILLAS, IN FRONT OF THE JUDGE'S HOUSE. NIGHT

Valentine's car moves slowly through the neighbourhood of villas. She finds the right number, stops the car, gets out. She presses the bell at the

gate. Somewhere far, inside the house, she hears the quiet buzz of the bell. The lights are on in the house, but nobody reacts to the bell. Valentine rings again. No reaction. She notices that the gate is slightly ajar. She pushes it open, crosses the small yard and knocks on the front door. Again nobody answers. Apprehensive, she half opens the door and enters.

INT. JUDGE'S HOUSE. NIGHT

The house is old, well furnished, although neglected.

> VALENTINE
> *(loudly)*
> Good evening . . . Hello . . .

Nobody answers. Valentine makes a move, crosses two lit rooms and a kitchen full of dirty dishes. The door to the living-room is open. Valentine stops at the threshold. A man is sitting in the living-room with his back to her. Valentine knocks on the doorframe, clears her throat. The man does not react. In the living-room we hear the hum and crackle of a radio, as if someone were listening to a wavelength which had long finished transmission. The green light indicating the wavelength is also on. Valentine approaches the man. He is elderly. His head is hanging off the armchair headrest and his eyes are closed. But he is not asleep. When Valentine, obviously worried, touches his shoulder, he opens his eyes, fully conscious. He looks at Valentine with indifference. Neither of them says anything for a while.

> Excuse me . . .

The man looks at her without a word.

> I'm sorry, the door was open . . .

No reaction. Valentine is no longer worried.

> I'm sorry, but I think I ran your dog over.

The man, who is a retired judge, frowns.

> Rita. An Alsatian, a large Alsatian.

The Judge answers calmly. He turns towards her.

JUDGE

That's possible. She's been missing since yesterday.

VALENTINE

She's on my seat, in my car. She's alive. I don't know what to do with her.

The Judge shrugs, he does not know either.

Would you like me to take her to hospital?

JUDGE

If you want to.

Valentine cannot understand the Judge's attitude.

VALENTINE

If I ran your daughter over, wouldn't you care either?

The Judge speaks more sharply than before.

JUDGE

I don't have a daughter, miss.

Valentine obviously wants to say something unpleasant, but the Judge beats her to it.

Go away.

Valentine leaves without a word, closes the living-room door. She is already in the kitchen when the Judge's unexpected yell reaches her.

(*off*)

Don't shut the door!

Surprised by the Judge's outburst, Valentine returns, opens the door again and sees that the Judge has got up from his armchair and is standing at the window with his back to her. A pair of wide, old-fashioned braces hold up his trousers. Valentine disappears in the darkness of the corridor.

EXT. IN FRONT OF THE JUDGE'S HOUSE. NIGHT

Valentine turns around angrily, slamming the gate. She sees the Judge in the window against the illuminated room. The Judge is not looking in her direction but Valentine takes half a step backwards, her face disappearing in the shadows. She opens the car door, touches the dog's head. She glances in the Judge's direction once more but he is no longer in the window.

INT. VETERINARY HOSPITAL – CASUALTY. NIGHT

Valentine leans forward on her plastic stool. Through the half-open opaque glass door, she sees the dog's face as she lies on a high bed or table. The dog is looking at her. We see the silhouettes of people treating her. The Doctor – a veterinary surgeon – opens the door wider, smiles at Valentine.

> DOCTOR
> Nothing's happened to her really. We've stitched up the wound. She's got a bit of bruising and has to rest for a few days. She's pregnant. Do you want to take her or leave her with us?

Valentine gets up. The dog immediately tries clumsily to get up so as to be nearer to her.

> VALENTINE
> I'll take her.

The Doctor is kind.

> DOCTOR
> We'll help you carry her to the car.

He leans out and shouts down the corridor.

> Marc!

Valentine reacts sharply to the name, looks in the direction from which the said Marc should be coming. An elderly, stout man appears down the corridor. Seeing him, Valentine loses all interest in the name Marc.

INT./EXT. VALENTINE'S FLAT. DAY

Morning. Valentine is in bed. She is holding the receiver to her ear, obviously amused. The bandaged dog is lying next to her on the red jacket.

MICHEL
(*off*)

Are you alone?

VALENTINE

No . . . And I didn't spend the night alone either.

Michel's voice becomes silent over the telephone. Only his breathing can be heard. Valentine brings her hand up to the dog's nose; the dog starts licking her.

He's licking me. Can you hear?

MICHEL
(*off*)

I can hear . . .

Valentine brings the receiver up to the dog.

VALENTINE

Say something to him. Well, go on . . .

The dog pricks up her ears, growls. Valentine takes the receiver. Laughs.

Did you hear that? I've got a dog.

MICHEL
(*off, with relief*)

A dog?

VALENTINE

A dog. I ran her over last night.

Only now does she realize that the joke was not funny for her partner.

I'm sorry.

MICHEL
(*off*)

That wasn't funny.

VALENTINE

No, it wasn't. Do you remember how we met?

She settles down more comfortably. She strokes the dog automatically. Michel does not quite understand Valentine's intentions.

MICHEL
(*off*)

I remember . . .

VALENTINE

If I hadn't taken a break right at that moment, we wouldn't have met.

MICHEL
(*off*)

No. Valentine . . . give the dog back.

VALENTINE

I tried. The owner doesn't want her.

MICHEL
(*off*)

Whose is it?

At that moment, we hear a car hoot at regular intervals outside. Valentine looks in the direction of the window.

VALENTINE

An alarm's gone off. It might be mine.

Valentine runs up to the window. Her small car on the street is flashing at regular intervals and hooting.

It's mine. Can you hold on? I'll just turn it off.

MICHEL
(off)

I can't, I'm in a hurry.

VALENTINE

I see.

She replaces the receiver.

INT./EXT. AUGUST'S FLAT. DAY

August also hears the regular hooting of the car. He raises his head from his desk where he is taking notes. He is wearing a shirt and braces. We see the book open where the gust of wind had opened it yesterday. August gets up and approaches the window. He opens it, leans out. He loses interest when he sees the small car hooting and flashing its lights while his jeep stands undisturbed. He glances at his watch, leans out further. Down the street an attractive woman is nearing his building. August raises his hand in greeting. A blonde, Karin, smiles at him and answers with a similar gesture. August closes the window, does not see the woman's (Valentine's) silhouette leaving her gate and getting into the flashing, hooting car. Her face is not distinguishable from this distance. Valentine switches off the alarm. August stretches himself. Judging by the stubble on his chin, the lamp lit by his desk, the number of empty coffee mugs and his unmade bed, he has not slept that night. He smiles and yawns. He quickly clears away the coffee mugs, spoons some food into the dog's dish – the dog starts eating straight away – and goes up to the intercom. He waits. When the buzzer sounds, he immediately presses the button, releasing the gate lock.

INT. VALENTINE'S FLAT. DAY

The dog wags her tail as soon as Valentine opens the front door. Valentine comes up to her, sits down on the floor and strokes the dog's head.

                              VALENTINE
     I ran you over. And what now?

The dog tilts her head. She seems to understand Valentine's problem.

INT. PHOTOGRAPHER'S STUDIO. DAY

*Valentine's face blowing a bubble of gum on a number of photographs.
The Photographer arranges the prints so that they can all be seen at the
same time. Some really are amusing. They both lean over the lit surface.
Valentine runs her finger above the photographs, considers them.
Finally, she brings it down on one of the photographs.*

                              VALENTINE
     I like this one.

                             PHOTOGRAPHER
     I picked that one, too. And this one in reserve . . .

He points to another photograph, also good. Valentine nods.

                             PHOTOGRAPHER
     Twenty-five feet by sixty-five.

*He smiles, imagining the effect of such a big enlargement. He is a
pleasant, fair young man.*

     People are going to recognize you in the street.

Valentine laughs.

                              VALENTINE
     Who?

                             PHOTOGRAPHER
     Anybody particular in mind? I will, that's for sure.

*The Photographer puts his arm around her, gives her a little hug. He
brings his face close to hers. When we think he is going to kiss her on the
lips, Valentine gently turns away. The Photographer turns her face back
towards him.*

                              VALENTINE
     It's not you.

The Photographer lets go of her. He gathers the photographs from the table top, switches off the bright light. He looks at her now dark face. He notices Valentine's bulging coat pocket.

> PHOTOGRAPHER
> Something's sticking out of your pocket.

Valentine pulls out a long, red leash.

> It's pretty. Red . . . What's it for?

> VALENTINE
> I've got a dog now.

EXT. IN FRONT OF VALENTINE'S FLAT. DAY

Valentine gets out of her car which is parked in front of her building. She approaches the newspaper stand and pulls her paper out from the pile. Something on the front page immediately strikes her. Holding the coin ready in her hand, she stops in her tracks and spreads the paper. She studies the photograph on the front page carefully. August emerges from the café, cigarette in his mouth, dog on its red leash. He passes Valentine, who, immersed in her reading, realizes, after a while, that she is still holding her coin. She enters the café.

INT. CAFÉ. DAY

Valentine inserts the coin into the slot, pulls the lever. Coloured pictures whirl by in the display window and stop, one after another, at three red cherries. The machine groans and a generous handful of coins spills out into the drawer below. The clanging of the money has drawn the attention of the Barman who now goes up to Valentine.

> BARMAN
> Oh, bad luck.

Valentine nods. She unenthusiastically gathers up two handfuls of coins and pours them into her pocket.

> VALENTINE
> I think I know why I've won.

The Barman is intrigued.

INT. VALENTINE'S FLAT. NIGHT

Valentine, still in her coat, goes up to a shelf where there is a large jar half full of coins. She takes the coins which she won in the café from her pocket and pours them into the jar. Rita tilts her head at the clatter. Not all the coins fit into the jar and some fall out on to the sideboard, one on to the floor. Valentine watches it for a while, then unwillingly spreads out the newspaper which she bought. There is a report on drug addicts on the front page. Several photographs of typical groups, a close-up of an arm full of injection scars, a few faces closer up. Valentine bends over one of the faces. She is interrupted by a knock on the door. She goes up to the door with the paper in her hand. A fat Neighbour, noisily chewing gum, stands in the doorway.

> NEIGHBOUR
> Good evening. You're back . . . The postman left some money for you.

He hands Valentine several banknotes and the receipt for a money order. Valentine looks at the remittance with surprise.

> VALENTINE
> Who can that be from?

The Neighbour shrugs, he does not know. Valentine reads the sender's name and still does not understand.

> NEIGHBOUR
> Have you read? The Turks are getting over the mountains again.

> VALENTINE
> Yes, I've read about it.

> NEIGHBOUR
> Pests.

The Neighbour notices the newspaper which Valentine is holding. He tilts his head.

> Isn't that your brother?

> VALENTINE
> Or someone who looks like him . . .

NEIGHBOUR
Not very nice . . . Does your family read this paper?

Valentine looks at him, wondering what is on his mind.

VALENTINE
I don't know.

She closes the door and, for a moment, stands motionless. She goes back to her room and lifts the telephone receiver. She searches in her notebook and taps out a number. A woman's voice answers.

WOMAN
(*off*)
Hello?

VALENTINE
May I speak to Marie, please.

Now we hear a girl's voice.

MARIE
(*off*)
Yes?

VALENTINE
Valentine. Are you going to be seeing Marc?

MARIE
(*off*)
Yes. Tonight probably.

VALENTINE
Tell him to call me. Doesn't matter what time.

Valentine replaces the receiver. She drops her hand, looks down. Rita is licking her fingers. Valentine smiles.

EXT. NEAR VALENTINE'S FLAT. DAY

There is a small park near Valentine's flat. It is Sunday morning and Valentine is talking to her dog here. Rita is on good form now, her bandage gone. A red leash is fastened to her collar. She is listening attentively to what Valentine is quietly saying to her.

VALENTINE

I'm going to let you go so that you can run around a bit. You won't run away, will you?

Rita looks at her lovingly, faithfully, calmly. Valentine unfastens the leash. As soon as she feels she is free, the dog immediately darts away. Initially, Valentine thinks that the dog is going to run a circle and return to her. She calls her in a friendly tone.

VALENTINE

Rita! Rita, come here!

But the dog does not react and runs on ahead without turning. Worried, Valentine follows Rita. Rita turns the corner. Valentine follows.

(*shouts*)

Riiita!

The dog is clearly running away. She runs across the church square and, to Valentine's despair, bursts into the church through the open door. Valentine stops in front of the church, waits for a moment. Seeing that the dog is not coming out, she goes inside.

INT. CHURCH. DAY

The church is quite large. A Mass is in progress. A dozen or so faithful have gathered. Valentine looks around. People in the pews turn towards her as her heels click on the floor. Dipping her hand in the holy water, Valentine crosses herself quickly. With the leash in her hand, she does not pay attention to the people any more, and quickly walks to the front. She stops before the altar. The red leash looks absurd. Valentine realizes this. She gathers courage and asks out loud – the Mass has already been interrupted as it is.

VALENTINE

I'm very sorry. But my dog's run away.

Following the priest's eyes – he has noticed something at the back of the church – Valentine turns around. Rita runs out of the church. Valentine genuflects, then quickly leaves the church.

EXT. NEAR VALENTINE'S FLAT. DAY

At the church corner, Valentine sees Rita disappear down the street. She now knows that she will not catch up with her. She runs in the direction of her car, which is parked outside her building. She searches in her pockets but does not find her keys. Furious, she waves her arm, runs into her gate. The camera slowly pans and on the opposite side of the street we see August leaving his building with his dog, his arm around Karin. The dog, on a red leash, tugs in the direction in which Rita has run away. August has to shorten the leash. They get into his jeep and drive away. The camera pans after the disappearing jeep right up to the moment when Valentine appears in frame, coming out of her gate with her car keys and leash in her hand. Her bag – with the usual newspaper sticking out of it – is slung over her shoulder. She gets into the car and drives off in the opposite direction to the jeep. Valentine drives towards the street down which Rita disappeared. At first she slows down at each crossroads, looking for the dog. Then she accelerates, realizing the futility of her efforts. She leaves her residential neighbourhood.

EXT. NEAR THE JUDGE'S HOUSE. DAY

Valentine enters the neighbourhood of villas. She finds the street she already knows, stops the car in front of the Judge's house. The gate is open, there is nobody in the garden. Valentine considers for a moment. She gets out of the car and goes up to the gate. She rings the bell. The front door opens. Rita appears in the doorway and, immediately behind her, the Judge. The dog looks at Valentine, wagging her tail. Valentine, reassured, does not go in. She speaks loudly so that the Judge can hear her from that distance.

> VALENTINE
>
> She's come back to you.

The Judge shrugs. He speaks equally loudly.

> JUDGE
>
> Call her. She's yours.

> VALENTINE
> (*half-heartedly*)
>
> Rita . . .

*The dog takes a dozen or so steps, quickly at first, and then stops
halfway down the path between the house and gate. Wagging her tail
restlessly, she looks once at the Judge, once at Valentine. It is an
amusing situation, Valentine smiles. She goes through the gate up to the
dog. The Judge, too, walks down the steps and approaches Rita from
the other side. In the end, they stand face to face with the dog between
them. Valentine opens her bag, rummages inside for a while and pulls
out several banknotes together with the remittance. She shows them to
the Judge.*

Did you send this?

The Judge nods.

> JUDGE
> For the dog's treatment.

> VALENTINE
> How did you know my . . .

The Judge interrupts her, waves his arm.

> JUDGE
> It wasn't hard.

Valentine hands him the money and remittance.

> VALENTINE
> You've no idea how much it costs. The treatment was 130
> francs, you sent me 600.

*She takes the vet's receipt from her bag and hands it to the Judge. The
Judge checks it meticulously. He nods, takes five hundred-franc notes for
himself and gives one to Valentine. He searches in his pocket for some
change but cannot find any.*

> JUDGE
> I'll go and find some change.

He moves to go, the dog following. Valentine stops them with a question.

> VALENTINE
> And what about Rita?

JUDGE

She's a very intelligent dog. Really. Take her.

VALENTINE

Don't you want her?

Unexpectedly – for the first time – the Judge smiles faintly.

JUDGE

I don't want anything.

Despite the smile, the confession sounds somewhat pretentious to Valentine.

VALENTINE

Then stop breathing.

The Judge reacts gravely.

JUDGE

Good idea.

He goes towards the house, up the steps. The dog stays at his foot. The Judge opens the door and disappears inside. Rita stays on the porch, wagging her tail at Valentine. Valentine waits for the Judge to return, but the door stays closed. Rita has concluded that the situation is normal and is sitting peacefully in front of the door. Valentine puts her hands in her pockets and takes a few steps towards the house. The wait continues. She shrugs and makes her way back to the car. By the fence, she turns and looks at the windows of the house. There is nobody there. Angry with herself, she calls loudly.

VALENTINE

Excuse me!

She goes back to the house and peers in the high-set ground-floor window. She has to stand on tiptoes to knock. No one reacts to the knocking; perhaps it is too weak.

(*loudly*)
Have you stopped breathing?

No reaction. Valentine walks up the steps and stands in front of the door. She hesitates a moment, then opens the door and goes inside. Rita stays outside.

225

INT. JUDGE'S HOUSE. DAY

On closing the door, Valentine hears voices coming from inside. These voices stop her for a moment in the corridor.

VALENTINE

Excuse me!

No one answers. Overcoming her natural sense of discretion, Valentine decides to go in further. She crosses the two rooms and the untidy kitchen again. The voices of men talking become clearer and clearer. She enters the living-room. The Judge is leaning forward in his armchair with his back to Valentine. There is nobody else in the room. The conversation between the two men is coming from the radio. It is a telephone conversation, accompanied by crackling and shrill electronic interference. Valentine listens, surprised. Neither the technical quality nor the content of the conversation sounds like a radio broadcast. Man I's voice is polite, calm and belongs to a forty-year-old. Man II's voice is clearly younger, unpleasantly soft, hysterical.

MAN I
(*off*)

I'm afraid I can't.

MAN II
(*off*)

If you don't come, you'll never see me again.

MAN I
(*off*)

It's Sunday, sir . . .

MAN II
(*off*)

Yesterday was Saturday. And you were with me. And please don't be so formal, I beg you . . .

MAN I
(*off*)

Hold on, I'll just go through to the other room.

We hear the sound of footsteps over the radio, a door closing. The Judge turns around, sensing Valentine's presence behind his back. He waves at thirty francs lying on the table. Valentine approaches.

VALENTINE

What are you doing?

Completely unexpectedly, the Judge chuckles with an unpleasant, inner laughter. A moment later, he raises his finger because we hear a man's voice again. Valentine, bewildered, falls silent and listens.

MAN I
(off)

Peter, I'm back.

MAN II
(off)

And I'm alone. And I want you to come over. I can't stand being alone. I can't . . .

MAN I
(off)

We said tomorrow, Peter . . .

MAN II
(off)

I missed you all night. I dreamt about you . . . You were standing in front of a mirror, naked . . .

What we suspected from the beginning now becomes clear – this is a private conversation on which we are eavesdropping. Valentine goes up to the radio and resolutely switches it off. She turns to the Judge.

VALENTINE

What are you doing?

JUDGE

Eavesdropping.

VALENTINE

What?

JUDGE

I'm listening to my neighbours' phone calls. You interrupted. It was interesting.

He chuckles briefly again.

You don't find it entertaining?

> VALENTINE
> It's disgusting.

> JUDGE
> Yes. What's more, it's illegal.

Valentine shakes her head incredulously. She goes up to the table, picks up the thirty francs and quickly leaves. The Judge's voice stops her.

One moment, please.

The Judge goes up to the radio and provocatively puts his hand on the knob.

You're so sure you're right, aren't you? Then do something.

> VALENTINE
> What?

The Judge turns the radio on very loudly.

> MAN II
> (*off*)
> . . . I open my mouth and imagine I'm kissing . . .

The Judge turns the radio off.

> VALENTINE
> What do you want from me? Do you want me to smash the radio in?

> JUDGE
> I'll buy myself a new one. Go see the man and tell him someone's listening to his conversations. And while you're at it, tell him it's me.

Valentine goes up to the Judge. She looks at him coldly.

> VALENTINE
> I will.

Through the window, the Judge points to a white house with a green roof.

228

> JUDGE

That's the house.

EXT./INT. NEAR THE JUDGE'S HOUSE. DAY

Valentine follows the path towards the house with the green roof. She rings the doorbell. After a moment, a thirty-year-old, pleasant, warm, well-dressed Woman opens the door. She smiles.

> WOMAN

Hello. Have you come to see us?

> VALENTINE

Hello. I wanted to see Mr . . .

Her voice peters out. The Woman is still pleasant.

> WOMAN

My husband? He's on the phone upstairs.

She opens the door wider.

Please, do come in . . .

INT. WOMAN'S HOUSE. DAY

Valentine takes a few steps inside. The Woman gestures to a chair by the door.

> WOMAN

Excuse me, I'll just turn the gas off.

The Woman goes off in the direction of the kitchen, disappears behind the door. Valentine looks around the house. The table in the middle of the room is laid for Sunday lunch. From the corridor, we see a nursery. Not believing her eyes, Valentine catches sight of a nine-year-old girl standing at her bedroom door with a telephone receiver at her ear, listening to her father's conversation. She notices Valentine and smiles pleasantly, just like her mother. Valentine abruptly backs away a step. The Woman approaches from within with a steaming teapot in her hand.

> WOMAN

Do sit down, he'll be finished in a minute. Caroline! . . .

She leans out in the direction of the nursery.

> Don't touch that phone. Daddy's talking!

Anxious, Valentine interrupts her.

VALENTINE
I'm sorry. I must have got the wrong address.

WOMAN
This is number twenty-two.

VALENTINE
Exactly. I'm sorry.

WOMAN
It's quite all right. It's been our pleasure.

Valentine backs out, the Woman shuts the door.

EXT. NEAR THE JUDGE'S HOUSE. DAY

Valentine quickly passes through the Judge's gate. We briefly see a jeep stop further down the road. Karin gets out, goes round to the driver's seat and kisses August who is sitting there. A dog cranes out of the window, whines and wags its tail in the direction of the Judge's house. Valentine does not look in that direction. Without stroking the fawning Rita, who is staring at August's dog, she runs down the path, annoyed, and enters forcibly.

INT. JUDGE'S HOUSE. DAY

Valentine enters the living-room. The radio is on again – we hear a Woman's voice.

WOMAN
(*off*)
. . . I advise you to go via Berne and Strasbourg, so as to avoid great . . .

MAN
(*off*)
Thank you very much.

WOMAN
(*off*)

Thank you. Goodbye.

We hear the click of a receiver being replaced and the quiet hum of the radio. Valentine walks up to the Judge. The Judge shrugs.

JUDGE
(*sarcastically*)

Well? Did you tell him?

Valentine speaks louder than usual.

VALENTINE

No. But I've come back . . .

We hear a kettle whistling. The Judge gets up, picks up a newspaper from the floor and hands it to Valentine.

JUDGE

You dropped . . .

Valentine checks – the newspaper which usually lies on the top in her bag is not there. The Judge goes out to the kitchen and switches the kettle off.

Make yourself some tea or coffee.

Valentine does not answer, so the Judge appears in the doorway with the steaming kettle in his hand.

Would you like something to drink?

VALENTINE

No.

(*raising her voice*)

No, I wouldn't. I came back . . . I came back to ask you something. Please don't do that any more.

The Judge tilts the kettle and the steaming water trickles to the floor.

JUDGE

I've done it all my life.

Valentine, shocked, watches the stream pouring from the kettle.

What?

The Judge does not reply.

You've been spilling water from your kettle?

The kettle is empty. The Judge takes it back to the kitchen. Valentine follows him and stands at the threshold of the dirty kitchen.

What did you do?

It is hard to find space for the kettle among all the dirty dishes so the Judge stands it on a pile of dishes, smashing a plate and glass.

Eavesdropped?

The Judge goes back to the room, passing Valentine in the doorway.

JUDGE
(*murmurs*)
You could put it that way.

VALENTINE
Jesus . . . what were you? A cop?

The Judge goes back and sits down in his armchair.

JUDGE
Worse. A judge.

Valentine comes closer and sits on the edge of her chair.

VALENTINE
A judge?

JUDGE
Haven't you seen a real judge before?

The Judge stretches his wide, old-fashioned braces and lets them go. The elastic smacks against his body. The Judge repeats the operation. This time he stretches the braces further. The snap of elastic. He stretches the braces one more time and holds the stretched elastic towards Valentine.

Would you like a go? It makes a lovely sound . . .

Valentine shakes her head in disgust. The Judge gently lets the braces go.

I don't really know what side I was on: the good or the bad. But here . . .

He indicates the radio.

. . . I know the truth more or less. It's a better point of view than in a courtroom.

Valentine shakes her head with conviction.

VALENTINE
No. Everyone's got a right to their secrets.

JUDGE
Of course . . . So why did you stop? Why didn't you tell him I'm spying?

He gets up and starts pacing around the room. He speaks louder than a moment ago, almost shouts.

Because you saw that he's got a lovely, sweet wife? And a lovely, sweet daughter? And you couldn't . . . You felt sorry or were you just afraid of doing any harm?

VALENTINE
Both, I suppose.

The Judge leans over Valentine. He lowers his voice.

JUDGE
Let me tell you how it really is. I can spy on him or not. You could have told them or not. But sooner or later he's going to jump out of that window anyway, or she's going to find out and there's going to be hell. At some stage, someone's going to tell his daughter. Maybe she's the one who's going to jump out of that window . . . What can we do about it?

Valentine lowers her head, averts her eyes. The Judge notices her condition.

Does this remind you of something?

VALENTINE
Yes . . .

234

JUDGE

What? Tell me.

Valentine explains unwillingly.

VALENTINE

A certain boy.

The Judge repeats emphatically, looking Valentine in the eyes.

JUDGE

A certain boy who . . . What? Found out that his mother was
a whore?

VALENTINE

Found out that he wasn't his father's son. He was fifteen.
That man's daughter there . . .

She points in the direction of the house with the green roof.

She already knows.

She moves as if to get up.

JUDGE

Don't move a minute.

*Valentine stops mid-movement. She looks at the Judge and he looks at
her without a word. After a long while, Valentine, confused, breaks the
silence.*

VALENTINE

Why?

JUDGE

The light is beautiful.

*Valentine smiles faintly to mask her embarrassment or perhaps slight
fear. At that moment, the sound of dialling comes through the radio.
The tone and a Woman's voice answering the phone.*

WOMAN'S VOICE
(*off*)

Good morning. Detailed weather report.

235

VOICE
(*off*)

Apparently you give an exact weather check for Europe. I
read an ad . . .

WOMAN'S VOICE
(*off*)

That's right.

VOICE
(*off*)

I'm driving to Turin tomorrow morning . . .

WOMAN'S VOICE
(*off*)

Turin. One moment, please . . .

The Judge turns to Valentine.

JUDGE

In this way I know what the weather's like all over Europe.

WOMAN'S VOICE
(*off*)

Up until Chamonix, the road is quite clear. Between
Chamonix and the tunnel, we forecast snowfalls in the
morning until about noon. The road may be slippery. Then
from there the road through to Turin is good. Please be
careful. It's best you leave before seven, that way you'll avoid
the snow.

VOICE
(*off*)

Thank you very much. It's a wonderful idea, this service.

WOMAN'S VOICE
(*off*)

Thank you. Goodbye.

The Judge gets up. Valentine looks up at him.

VALENTINE

That's a swindle. You're not paying for the weather forecast.

236

JUDGE

True enough. It didn't occur to me . . . But there's another reason why I'm listening to her phone . . . Aha . . .

The Judge lifts his finger, listens. The sound of dialling and a connection being made comes through the radio. The same Woman answers.

WOMAN'S VOICE
(off)

Good morning. Detailed weather report.

MAN'S VOICE
(off)

It's me. Did you manage to get some sleep?

WOMAN'S VOICE
(off)

A little. I didn't say anything but it was wonderful. We've never made love so passionately before.

MAN'S VOICE
(off)

Yes, Karin. I woke up in the morning when you were still asleep. You looked just like a little child.

The Judge does not notice but, at this point in the conversation, Valentine puts her fingers in her ears and closes her eyes. She does not do this ostentatiously but effectively.

WOMAN'S VOICE
(off, light-heartedly)

I'm older than you.

MAN'S VOICE
(off)

Only a year.

WOMAN'S VOICE
(off)

Two.

MAN'S VOICE
(off)

Everything all right?

WOMAN'S VOICE
(*off*)

Two calls all of a sudden. It's hard to make a living out of detailed weather reports. I love you.

MAN'S VOICE
(*off*)

Karin . . . I called you because I suddenly got scared.

WOMAN'S VOICE
(*off*)

Of the exam?

MAN'S VOICE
(*off*)

No. The future. Of what I'm going to be doing.

A moment's silence.

WOMAN'S VOICE
(*off, gaily*)

You wouldn't like to take me bowling, would you?

MAN'S VOICE
(*off*)

I've just opened all my books . . . Have you got a coin?

WOMAN'S VOICE
(*off*)

I do . . .

MAN'S VOICE
(*off*)

Toss it. Tails it's bowling, heads Penal Code.

The Judge takes a coin from his pocket, tosses and catches it on his open palm. The five-franc piece falls tails up. The Judge smiles and glances at Valentine who has been blocking her ears all the time. We hear the sound effects of the same scene over the radio.

WOMAN'S VOICE
(*off*)

Tails. It's bowling.

MAN'S VOICE
(*off*)

I'll sit another hour or two, then call you.

WOMAN'S VOICE
(*off*)

Or I you.

The click of a receiver being replaced. The Judge turns to Valentine. He gets up and lightly taps her on the shoulder. Valentine opens her eyes, takes her fingers from her ears.

JUDGE

You didn't listen?

Valentine shakes her head.

Pity. It was very romantic.

VALENTINE

I heard the beginning. They're in love.

JUDGE

Ye-e-es . . . He thinks he's in seventh heaven, but any minute now he's going to come crashing down to earth.

VALENTINE

Nobody knows that.

The Judge nods, as if he knows.

JUDGE

He hasn't met the right woman. That often happens. It's funny . . . He drives the car I dreamt of having when I was his age.

VALENTINE

What's the car got to do with it?

JUDGE

Not much. Only that he bought it because she likes cars like that. I sometimes watch them from my window . . .

He walks up to the window, looks out and obviously notices something because he faintly smiles.

You think I'm a bastard, don't you?

VALENTINE

Yes.

JUDGE

Take a look.

Valentine unwillingly goes to the window. In the neighbouring garden, a middle-aged, good-looking man is talking through a mobile phone. He is explaining something energetically and giving out instructions.

That guy bought his phone in Japan. It's on a different wavelength so I can't pick it up on my radio. Pity. I think that half the heroin sold in Geneva goes through his hands.

Valentine watches the man with sudden interest.

We have nothing on him. He doesn't deal in retail.

The Judge notices Valentine's interest.

You fancy him?

VALENTINE

Very much.

JUDGE

Shall I call him?

The Judge taps on the pane – not too loudly. The man does not hear. The Judge wants to tap harder.

VALENTINE
(*shouts*)

No!

The Judge looks at her, pretending to be surprised.

Have you got his number?

The Judge reaches for the telephone directory and flicks through the pages. Meanwhile, the man finishes his conversation. He is annoyed at something. The Judge finds his number, taps it out and hands Valentine the cordless telephone. We hear the tone. The man is walking towards his house; the sound of his phone stops him. He brings the receiver to his ear.

You deserve to die.

She turns the phone off. For a while, the man stands bewildered by what he has just heard. He looks around anxiously, hides the telephone aerial. Then he goes to his house at a trot. Valentine hands the receiver to the Judge.

VALENTINE
Jesus, what have I done . . .?

JUDGE
You might have been overheard. Nearly everyone's got phones like that around here. And with topography like this conversations can be heard over the radio . . . I think the wavelengths bounce off those mountains.

He indicates a stretch of Alps visible from the window. He takes out an old fountain pen, shakes the ink down several times and notes something on a scrap of paper.

JUDGE
It's been drying up for years . . .

He hands Valentine the piece of paper.

I've noted down his number for you. If you want to say something nasty to him, you can.

He goes up to the radio and fiddles with the knob for a while. We hear isolated words or music from various radio stations. After a while, the Judge tunes into another telephone conversation.

Next programme. Not very interesting.

We hear the voice of a sick, very Old Woman.

OLD WOMAN
(*off*)
. . . and I went to bed but couldn't sleep. I kept tossing and turning for hours. It kept hurting all the time. Still does. I didn't do any shopping . . .

YOUNG WOMAN
(*off*)
That's annoying for you, Mum.

OLD WOMAN
(*off*)

I haven't got any milk, no bread even . . .

The Young Woman interrupts her mother.

YOUNG WOMAN
(*off*)

But you do, Mum. I bought lots and put it in the freezer.

OLD WOMAN
(*off*)

I've eaten it all.

YOUNG WOMAN
(*off*)

Stop, Mum! You haven't eaten seven loaves of bread in four days! I can't stand . . .

The Judge switches off the radio. He turns to Valentine. With her eyes wide-open and with almost a physical sense of pain, she is sitting huddled up in her chair.

JUDGE

Do you want to do her shopping? You'd feel better.

VALENTINE
(*helplessly*)

Maybe she'd feel better?

The Judge shakes his head doubtfully.

JUDGE

Why did you pick Rita up from the street?

For Valentine it is obvious.

VALENTINE

Because I'd run her over. She was hurt and bleeding.

JUDGE

You'd still be feeling guilty if you'd left her there. Maybe you'd even dream of the dog with her head all crushed in.

Valentine has to admit he is right.

VALENTINE

Yes . . .

JUDGE

So who did you do it for? Don't do that old woman's shopping. She's got everything. What she really wants is to see her daughter. But the daughter doesn't want to. She came here at least five times when her mother was pretending to have a heart attack. When she dies, I'm going to have to call her daughter because she won't believe it any more. She won't believe . . .

He shrugs. Valentine gets up. She tries to shake off the feeling of oppression. She looks at the Judge with wide-open eyes.

VALENTINE

You're wrong.

JUDGE

About what?

VALENTINE

About everything. You're wrong about everything. People aren't bad, it's not true.

Maybe she is naive and childish in her protest; she is certainly sincere.

JUDGE

They are.

VALENTINE

No! No . . . Sometimes they're just too weak . . .

If Valentine were not so proud, she would burst out crying. The Judge watches her attentively.

JUDGE

That boy who found out his father wasn't his father. Is he your boyfriend or brother?

VALENTINE

Brother.

JUDGE

How old is he?

> VALENTINE

Sixteen.

> JUDGE

How long has he been shooting up?

> VALENTINE

How do you know?

> JUDGE

It wasn't hard to guess.

> VALENTINE

I can only pity you.

She abruptly leaves the room. The Judge turns after her with a request or a question in his eyes. Valentine stops for a moment by the door.

> (*quietly*)

I don't know if you know. Your dog is going to have puppies.

Before the Judge has time to react, Valentine leaves the room and the house.

INT. CAR INTERIOR. DUSK

Valentine drives home. She doesn't have to hold back or be ashamed any more. Tears roll down her face, one after another. She wipes them, but cannot or does not want to stop them.

EXT. NEAR VALENTINE'S FLAT. DUSK

Valentine's car stops in front of her house. She gets out, still in tears. She locks the car and walks towards her gate. The camera leaves her, wanders across the façades and comes to August's already illuminated window.

INT. AUGUST'S FLAT. DUSK

Books and notes lie spread out on the table, a small desk lamp is alight. It looks as if no one is in. The telephone rings. The camera leaves the telephone and tracks to the window. It tracks out of the window and looks down on to the street. August is running out of the small Joseph

*café – already familiar to us – with a carton of Marlboros in his hand.
In shirt and braces, he runs across the street into his gate. The camera
returns to the room and, after a while, we see August enter. His black
dog greets him in the doorway as if after a week's absence. August tears
the carton open, pulls out a packet and takes out a cigarette. He
shudders – it must have been cold outside. He lights up with pleasure.
He picks up the telephone and punches out a number. We hear an
engaged tone. August smiles and replaces the receiver.*

INT. VALENTINE'S FLAT. NIGHT

*Valentine takes out the redundant red leash from her coat pocket.
Slowly, she drops it into the bin. Her eyes are still moist and swollen.
Suddenly anxious, she goes up to the telephone and dials.*

>   MOTHER
>   (*off*)
> Hello?

>   VALENTINE
> It's Valentine, Mum.

>   MOTHER
>   (*off*)
> Valentine . . . Hello darling.

>   VALENTINE
> How are you, Mum? Did Marc come?

>   MOTHER
>   (*off*)
> Two days ago. With his girlfriend. He's got a lovely girl. Do
> you know her?

Valentine breathes a sigh of relief.

>   VALENTINE
> I do. It's Marie.

>   MOTHER
>   (*off*)
> We're sitting here, chatting . . . They're watching TV now.

Valentine's mood improves.

VALENTINE

Pity, I can't be there.

MOTHER
(*off*)

It is a pity. It's like the old days. Your brother is a good boy, isn't he?

VALENTINE

He is. Can I talk to him for a moment?

MOTHER
(*off*)

Marc! He's just coming.

VALENTINE

Call me, Mum. Lots of love.

MARC
(*off*)

Hi, Valentine.

VALENTINE

Hi. Thanks for going there.

MARC
(*off*)

At your service. We're going back tomorrow. I can't stand it.

VALENTINE

Has Mum seen the paper?

MARC
(*off*)

I don't think so. Even if she had . . . It wouldn't occur to her.

VALENTINE

You're right. You should go home.

MARC
(*off*)

'Bye.

Valentine replaces the receiver. Her eyes are still swollen. She watches the phone and begs quietly.

VALENTINE

Call me, Michel. Please, call me . . .

The telephone rings immediately. Valentine sighs, gathers herself together, picks up the receiver.

PHOTOGRAPHER
(off; energetic)

Valentine? Have you seen the photo?

VALENTINE

What? Is that you, Jacques?

PHOTOGRAPHER
(off)

It's me, it's me. It's turned out great. Haven't you seen it?

VALENTINE

No . . . I forgot. I had a tough day.

PHOTOGRAPHER
(off)

Then come and join us. It's fun. It'll relax you . . .

VALENTINE

Where?

INT. BOWLING ALLEY. NIGHT

Valentine's hand chooses a large, plastic bowling ball. Her fingers slip into the purpose-made holes. Valentine feels the weight of the ball. She then gathers speed and throws. The bowling ball rolls down the centre of the alley and Valentine, bent over in a strange position after her throw, waits for the result. The pins scatter – only one or two are left standing. Several people, among them the Photographer, cheer Valentine on as, smiling, she returns for the next bowl. She gathers speed, throws and while she waits, in her strange, bent-over position again, the camera moves at right angles across the other alleys. There are several people at each stand – throwing, drinking beer, jotting down results. A dozen or so yards further down is the last stand. There is nobody there. An empty packet of Marlboro lies on the table, smoke coils up from an abandoned cigarette not stubbed out in the ashtray. We watch this for a while.

INT. JUDGE'S HOUSE. NIGHT

Five newly born puppies are fighting for Rita's teats. They push their way through clumsily, one over the other, and only settle down when they can all suck. The bitch closes her eyes, tired. The Judge, with a bright smile we have not seen on his face before, watches this scene which is taking place in a cot built of boards. Something occurs to him quite unexpectedly. He gets up from the cot and goes up to his desk. He takes out several sheets of paper and a pile of envelopes. He thinks it over for a moment and counts out a dozen or so envelopes. He sits down, searches for his pen, finds it under a pile of newspapers on his desk. There is also a large old-fashioned gramophone record among the newspapers. A typical engraving from the end of the eighteenth century of a man's portrait features on the record sleeve. The Judge puts the record aside, unscrews the pen, puts it to paper. We know the pen. It does not write. The Judge shakes the ink down several times; still the pen does not write. The Judge impatiently searches for something on his desk. He finds a pencil with a broken point. He goes to the kitchen and sharpens the pencil with a dirty knife. He returns to the desk and writes the date in the left-hand corner of the first sheet of paper. After a moment's consideration, he starts to print his name, surname and address.

EXT. CITY STREET. DAY

The wind blows around the enormous enlargement of Valentine's photograph on which she is blowing a bubble of gum and laughing. The photograph has been printed over the entire surface of a canvas covering the scaffolding of a multi-storeyed building which is under renovation in the centre of town. August, wearing a suit and tie, is sitting in his car, waiting for the lights to change. Surprised, he leans forward, noticing something which probably had not been there the day before. He knows the building – which is now surrounded by scaffolding and the canvas – very well. The gusts of wind cause Valentine's face to frown, to change constantly, giving the still photograph the impression of coming to life. Her smile is contagious, the changing expressions are amusing and August smiles at the photograph. He is so lost in thought that he does not notice the lights change. It takes a few emphatic hoots from the cars behind for August to turn away from the photograph, glance at his watch and move off. As it drives past the building under renovation,

August's jeep, like all the other cars, appears tiny against the enormous photograph. He parks outside the building. The wind blows the clouds away and the photograph suddenly becomes brighter as the morning sun falls on it at an angle.

EXT. IN FRONT OF THE BUILDING. DAY

The weather has changed; it is cloudy again. Wide steps lead down from the building next door to the one under renovation, the one with Valentine's photograph. Several people are waiting at these steps. The atmosphere is a little like in front of a school during final exams. The doors open and August, in suit and tie as before, appears. He is holding several books in his hand. He looks around and catches sight of Karin waiting below. He walks down with a serious expression. Just as he reaches Karin, he smiles joyfully and throws the books and notes he was holding in the air. Karin hugs him and he hugs Karin.

> KARIN
> I knew you'd pass. Well done! Did you get that question?

August does not quite understand.

> From the book you dropped in the road . . . You told me about it.

August remembers. Smiles, nods. He raises his eyes over Karin's shoulders. Just above it, he sees Valentine's face at a very acute angle. Karin pushes him at arm's length and looks at him proudly. They are both smiling, happy. August thinks better of it and, still smiling, bends to gather his scattered books; they might still prove useful. Karin squats down next to him and pulls out a small present from her bag. She hands it to August. It is a fountain pen of high quality. August opens and closes the pen. He grows unexpectedly thoughtful, loses his good mood. Karin notices the change.

> Don't you like it?

> AUGUST
> It's beautiful. What's the first verdict I sign with it going to be?

Karin takes him by the arm and they walk away. Above them, Valentine's photograph appears. The sun emerges from behind the clouds again.

249

INT. STAIRWELL TO VALENTINE'S FLAT. NIGHT

Valentine reaches her door, mechanically puts the key in the keyhole, but the key will not go in. Surprised, Valentine tries once more – in vain. She examines the lock and discovers a ball of chewing-gum pressed into the keyhole. She pulls the gum away with distaste. At that moment, she hears the telephone ring in her flat. She inserts the key but it only goes in halfway. The telephone continues ringing. Valentine renews her futile efforts to unlock the door. The telephone stops. Valentine, furious at the practical joke, knocks on her neighbour's door. Her fat, forty-year-old neighbour opens it. He is out of breath from coming to the door. He smiles pleasantly at Valentine.

VALENTINE

Hello . . . I'm sorry to bother you but someone's played an idiotic joke on me. I can't get in.

NEIGHBOUR

It's those Turkish kids. They're all over the place.

VALENTINE

I've no idea. Someone's stuck chewing-gum in my lock.

The Neighbour rolls out of his door and examines Valentine's lock. He thinks it over with a serious expression. His face brightens.

NEIGHBOUR

Tweezers.

Valentine does not quite know what he means. The Neighbour pulls a complicated Swiss army knife from his pocket. It has a pair of tweezers. He plunges them into the keyhole and, fiddling with precision, pulls out the remainder of the chewing-gum. Pleased with himself, he hands it to Valentine.

It's the Turks, all right.

He smiles broadly.

They must've seen your latest ad.

VALENTINE

Thank you.

The Neighbour rolls home. Valentine opens the door – the key slips in smoothly now, as usual.

INT. VALENTINE'S FLAT. NIGHT

As soon as Valentine has closed the door, the telephone rings again. Valentine, still in her coat, picks up the receiver.

VALENTINE

Hello . . .

MICHEL
(off)

It's me. Good evening.

VALENTINE

Hi, Michel.

MICHEL
(off)

I called a minute ago but nobody answered.

VALENTINE

Someone stuck some gum up my lock. I couldn't get in. I heard the phone ring.

MICHEL
(off)

Gum?

VALENTINE

Chewing-gum. I did an ad for chewing-gum. That must be why.

MICHEL
(off)

I told you. You shouldn't be doing this. They're using you . . .

VALENTINE

Michel . . .

MICHEL
(*off*)

I'm not saying anything.

VALENTINE

I just want a bit of peace, Michel. I want a peaceful life . . .

MICHEL
(*off*)

You won't get it from me. You've picked the wrong guy.

A moment's silence.

Have you met someone else?

VALENTINE

No. I'm waiting for you, Michel.

A moment's silence.

MICHEL
(*off*)

Why didn't you pick up the phone when I called earlier?

VALENTINE

I told you. I was standing in front of the door and couldn't
get in.

MICHEL
(*off*)

I see.

VALENTINE

How are things with you?

MICHEL
(*off*)

I'm off to Hungary next week. What're you doing?

VALENTINE

Going to bed.

MICHEL
(*off*)

Go on then. Go!

Valentine, hurt, does not say anything for a while. Michel does not speak either.

VALENTINE

Are you there?

Silence.

Michel, are you there?

Nobody answers. Valentine waits a moment longer and replaces the receiver.

(*murmurs*)

Jesus . . . Not again.

She takes off her coat, disappears into the bathroom. She takes off her blouse, keeping her bra on. She turns on the shower. The telephone rings again. Valentine runs into the room.

Hello.

MICHEL
(*off*)

Well, are you asleep?

VALENTINE

No, I'm not.

MICHEL
(*off*)

Then go to bed. Are you in bed?

VALENTINE

No. I've put the shower on. I'm getting undressed.

MICHEL
(*off*)

Anyone helping you?

This time Valentine stays silent.

Valentine . . . Valentine, are you there?

VALENTINE

No. Goodnight.

She replaces the receiver.

INT. COURT CORRIDOR. DAY

The Judge is sitting on a bench by a window in the corridor. We can easily guess that he is alone – on the other side of the closed, wide courtroom doors, dozens of people are milling around. Among them there is the Old Woman with a walking stick, supported by her Daughter, the pleasant Woman whom Valentine met, her Husband and Daughter, whom we also know. There is the Man whom the Judge described as a drug dealer and another dozen or so people. They sit or stand. Two Lawyers wander around among them, talking quietly and glancing at the Judge from time to time. Karin is sitting on a bench. The Judge looks at her attentively for a moment. Karin leans forward a little. She meets the eyes of a well-built Man whom she clearly does not know. The Man smiles at her, realizing that she has noticed him. Karin averts her eyes. The Man approaches her and introduces himself. The Judge, watching this tiny episode, half closes his eyes. At that moment, the courtroom door opens and the Court Usher stands at the threshold.

> COURT USHER
> *(loudly)*
> A civil hearing. The inhabitants of district X against Joseph Kern. Please enter the courtroom.

He moves aside and everybody enters. After a moment, the Judge, too, gets up and disappears through the courtroom door.

INT. MUSIC SHOP. DAY

Valentine, with large headphones over her ears, is listening to music in a music shop. It is crowded, all the stands with headphones are occupied. The stands are arranged in several rows so that the listeners stand with their backs to each other. Valentine clearly likes the music she has chosen. It is classical, piercing, with a beautiful, high-pitched, female voice singing in Dutch. A man, his arm around a woman, is standing right next to Valentine with his back to her. The camera tracks around the listening Valentine, passes by a boy in a sports jacket listening to heavy metal and slowly comes to the man standing behind Valentine. It is August with his arm around Karin. They are both listening to the finale of the same concert as Valentine. Karin is not particularly keen,

*August likes the music. They take their headphones off and both walk
off towards the cash register. The camera returns to Valentine – now
she, too, is coming to the end of the concert. She checks the number of
the disc she was listening to and the composer's name on the information
sheet. She removes her headphones and hands them over to the girl
waiting for her turn. She walks up to the cash register which August
and Karin have just left on their way out. Valentine smiles at the Shop
Assistant.*

VALENTINE

Number 432, please. Van den Budenmayer. Did I pronounce
it right?

SHOP ASSISTANT

You did.

*He searches for the disc on the shelf with classical music and returns to
Valentine with the disc in his hand.*

SHOP ASSISTANT

Is this the one?

Valentine nods. The Shop Assistant opens the disc sleeve – it is empty. A

typical reproduction of an engraving from the end of the eighteenth century is on the sleeve.

> SHOP ASSISTANT
> I've just sold the last one.

Valentine pulls a disappointed face. She automatically glances at the door. The door is closing behind August – we see his back and his arm wrapped around Karin. Valentine turns back to the Shop Assistant when he speaks to her.

> SHOP ASSISTANT
> I'll be getting some more this afternoon. I can put one aside for you if you can't come in.

> VALENTINE
> Thanks. I'll pop in this afternoon.

EXT. NEAR THE JUDGE'S HOUSE. DAY

A van, equipped with aerials and a dish trapping radio wavelengths on its roof makes its way through the roads of the villa neighbourhood where the Judge lives. We see the houses, villas and the chain of Alps through the revolving dish aerial. Every now and again the aerial comes to a standstill, as does the van. We hear quickened, electronic tones; a moment later the van moves off. We easily recognize the Judge's house, the white house with a green roof and, near by, a large building with several apartments. The aerial turns back and forth rhythmically. It stops again, catching tones which interest the technicians. The van comes to a standstill.

INT. BALLET STUDIO. DAY

Exhausted, sweaty Girls – clearly after a hard bout of ballet exercises – are resting in various positions. Valentine, large patches of sweat on her T-shirt, is lying on a low bench. She is breathing hard, a bottle of mineral water at her side. The Girls' handbags and plastic bags hang on window sills and ladder rungs. Valentine rolls on to her back, looks up. She notices something which unexpectedly catches her attention. She pulls herself up, stretches her arm out. A newspaper is sticking out from the bag hanging over the bar. We see the fragment of a headline of which Valentine can only read: '–ESTED JUDGE'.

VALENTINE

Whose paper is that?

The Girl sitting next to her, bent in half, glances at the bag.

GIRL

Yours.

The laughter of several tired Girls. Valentine, too, smiles. She pulls the paper from the bag. Opens it. On the last page she sees a large, sensationalist headline: 'SENSATION IN DISTRICT X. RETIRED JUDGE EAVESDROPPING ON HIS NEIGHBOURS' TELEPHONE CONVERSATIONS FOR YEARS'. Valentine reads the first few sentences of the article and lowers the paper. She smiles unpleasantly, but in a moment the smile abruptly disappears. She jumps up and quickly collects her belongings. She runs out of the hall.

INT./EXT. IN FRONT OF THE JUDGE'S HOUSE. DAY

The front door opens abruptly. Valentine stands at the door, the paper in her hand. The Judge, who has opened the door, looks at her with surprise but no smile. Valentine does not know where to start.

VALENTINE

I've come . . . I read about you in the paper. I wanted you to know that I didn't tell a soul.

JUDGE

I know.

VALENTINE

No one. Not the police, no one.

JUDGE

I know.

Valentine makes as if to go.

I know who it was.

Valentine stops.

> **VALENTINE**
> (*with curiosity*)

Who?

> **JUDGE**

It was me.

Valentine does not understand. She shakes her head. The Judge smiles unexpectedly.

> You asked me to. Do you want to come in? I've got
> something to show you . . .

He opens the door wider.

INT. JUDGE'S HOUSE. DAY

The Judge leads Valentine through a large room to the bedroom. A part of the bedroom has been partitioned off by boards and forms a cot where Rita and her newly born pups are lying. Their hunger satisfied, they lie in the most varied, amusing and touching positions. The exhausted Rita, seeing Valentine lean over, wags her tail a little. Valentine pours over them, stretches her hand out, retracts it. Although she may want to stroke the bitch or her puppies, she does not do so. The Judge, who stopped in the doorway, returns to the living-room, goes to a shelf and takes down several books. A bottle stands hidden behind them. The Judge pulls it out and finds two glasses. He returns to the bedroom door.

> **JUDGE**
> Would you like some pear brandy? I've had it for ages but I've
> never had an occasion until now.

Valentine rises from the cotside. The Judge hands her a glass, fills it.

> My health.

They drink. Valentine is not used to hard liquor. She chokes, then catches her breath.

> **VALENTINE**
> Why did you do it?

> **JUDGE**
> Why did I turn myself in?

258

VALENTINE

Yes.

JUDGE

I wanted to see what you'd do when you saw it in your paper.

The Judge points to the paper which Valentine is still holding in her hand.

VALENTINE

Did you think I'd come?

JUDGE

I thought you might, after our last conversation.

VALENTINE

Why?

The Judge shrugs helplessly.

Do you expect something from me?

JUDGE

Yes.

They are still standing at the bedroom door. The Judge straightens his arms so that his hands rest on the doorframe. In this way there is no way out of the bedroom. Valentine backs away a step.

JUDGE

You spoke of pity when you left here last time. Afterwards, I realized you were talking about disgust.

He lowers his arms and walks away further into the room. He stops in the middle of it.

Valentine . . . will you sit down for a minute?

Valentine hesitates a while. With the glass in her hand, she comes and sits on the chair where she sat before. The Judge sits in his armchair.

Are you going to give me a smile?

Valentine looks at him tensely, then, after a while, smiles gently. She lowers her eyes. The Judge gets up and pours her another tiny glass of pear brandy.

Did you cry after our last talk?

                    VALENTINE
I did.

                    JUDGE
And I switched the radio off. Then I sat at my desk. The ink
ran out of my old pen, the one I'd used all my life. I found a
pencil, sharpened it and wrote letters to my neighbours and
the police. I posted them that same night. There's a postbox
here, near by. You were sleeping soundly.

                    VALENTINE
I wasn't sleeping. I went bowling.

The Judge chuckles, briefly and unexpectedly.

                    JUDGE
Bowling? Do you remember that couple's conversation . . .
that boy and girl?

Valentine smiles.

260

VALENTINE

We listened in to it together.

JUDGE

They wanted to have some fun, too. That same night. Maybe
you were right next to them.

VALENTINE

Maybe . . .

JUDGE

I used to spend hours playing billiards at one time. I wasn't
much good. Once I took a clumsy shot. The ball fell off the
table straight into a large glass. We couldn't get it out. And
had to break the glass . . .

*He chuckles at the thought. Valentine is lost in her own thoughts for a
moment and does not take part in the story of the billiard ball.*

What are you thinking about?

VALENTINE

About that boy and girl. You didn't like her.

JUDGE

I was right. It's ending now.

Valentine looks at him uneasily.

VALENTINE

You look pleased about it. You didn't have a hand in it, did
you?

*The Judge gets up from his armchair, takes a few steps across the living-
room and stops behind Valentine's chair. Valentine follows him with her
eyes and now has to turn her head in order to see him.*

Did you?

JUDGE

Because of my eavesdropping and turning myself in, that girl
met a certain man.

INT. COURTS. DAY

August punches out a number at a public telephone. He waits. No one answers. He waits a long time, too long. He then hangs up and rests his head on his hand. He is worried, clenches his jaw. He glances at his watch, leaves the phone box. He walks down the long corridor and only now remembers that his gown is slung over his shoulder. Nearing one of many doors, without stopping, he pulls his gown on. He straightens the lapels, opens the door, goes inside. For a split second, we see a room with case files spread out and several people waiting for August. He shuts the door.

INT. JUDGE'S HOUSE. DUSK/NIGHT

It is growing dark outside. Valentine is telling the Judge something. He is sitting in the falling dusk, his face turned down. She finishes her sentence.

> VALENTINE
> . . . she's been alone ever since. I asked my brother to go and see her. He went and lasted three days. I'm going to England in a week's time. I don't know for how long. I'll be leaving Mum and him. And he's getting in deeper and deeper every day. I shouldn't be going.

She loses herself in thought.

> JUDGE
> Yes, you should. It's your destiny. The only one you've got. You can't live your brother's life.

> VALENTINE
> I love him. If there was anything I could do, anything . . .

> JUDGE
> You can. Just be.

Valentine doubts such a simple solution.

> VALENTINE
> What do you mean?

> JUDGE
> Exactly that: be.

A moment's silence. The Judge smiles at his own thoughts.

Do you like flying?

                    VALENTINE

No.

                    JUDGE

Take the ferry.

                    VALENTINE

I've never taken . . .

                    JUDGE

It's cheaper. And healthier.

                    VALENTINE

Good idea.

                    JUDGE

Maybe I turned myself in so that I'd have an idea you liked?

*The Judge raises his half-full glass. He drinks. Valentine copies him.
Her glass, too, is half-full. The bottle on the table is nearly full. This
time Valentine does not shudder as she drinks.*

You've taken to it?

                    VALENTINE

Yes.

                    JUDGE

It's my birthday today.

                    VALENTINE

I didn't know. I wish you . . . what shall I wish you? Peace?

                    JUDGE

That's a good wish.

He looks at his watch.

Thirty-five years ago, at this time, at three in the afternoon, I
acquitted a certain sailor. It was one of my first big cases. It
was a difficult time in my life. It's only recently that I realized
I'd made a mistake. He was guilty.

He gets up and switches on the big lamp standing on his desk. For a split second, the bulb lights up very brightly, then dies. The Judge unscrews the bulb and examines it against the fading light of the window.

I don't think I've got a spare one.

He stands a chair under the chandelier hanging from the ceiling and unscrews a bulb from it. He screws it into the lamp on the desk, switches it on. Valentine blinks, it has suddenly become very bright.

VALENTINE
What happened to him?

JUDGE
I did my own investigation. He got married. Has three children and now a grandson, too. They love him. He pays his taxes. All the trees he planted in front of his house have taken root and give fruit every year.

Valentine watches the Judge wide-eyed.

VALENTINE
That means you did the right thing. Good. Can't you see that?

JUDGE
As far as judiciary skills are concerned, I committed a very grave error.

Valentine stands up, almost shouts.

VALENTINE
You saved him!

JUDGE
Let's say . . . But just think: how many others could I have acquitted? Even though they may have been guilty? I've handed out hundreds of verdicts, but have I ever got to the truth? Is there such a thing as truth? And even if there is, and I've found it, then what for? Judging, sentencing . . . the very feeling of being able to decide what the truth is and what isn't . . . Now, I think it's lack of humility.

264

VALENTINE

Vanity?

JUDGE

Vanity.

He considers what he has just said. They don't say anything for a while.

VALENTINE

Pour me another drop will you?

The Judge tips the bottle, pours some pear brandy into both glasses. Valentine raises hers.

Your health. If I were to stand in front of a court . . . Do you think there are any judges like you left today?

They take a sip. The Judge smiles.

JUDGE

You won't stand in front of any court. Courts don't deal in innocence, they deal in guilt and punishment.

There is a loud crack and a stone falls into the middle of the room. The rest of the large window pane through which the stone flew in crashes to the floor with the tinkle of smashed glass. Valentine automatically curls up, frightened. The Judge is perfectly calm. He waves his hand at the broken window.

See that? That's the sixth window . . . Even though they've already changed the wavelength and I can't eavesdrop any more.

Valentine gets up, goes to the kitchen, opens a cupboard.

VALENTINE
(*loudly*)

Where's the broom?

Before hearing the answer, she finds it standing in the cupboard corner.

JUDGE

In the corner of the cupboard, at the bottom.

Valentine returns to the room, sweeps up the scattered glass. She also wants to put the stone into the dustpan, but the Judge picks it up and places it on a shelf alongside other stones which had been thrown in earlier. Meanwhile, we hear Valentine throw the glass into the bin. She returns to the room. The Judge is standing in his favourite position by the window. A cool evening breeze drifts in through the hole in the window.

VALENTINE

Aren't you scared?

The Judge shakes his head, he is not scared. He turns to face Valentine, sits on the sill.

JUDGE

I wonder what I'd do in their place.

He shrugs.

The same.

VALENTINE

You'd throw stones?

JUDGE

No doubt I would, if I were in their place. The same goes for all those I judged. With their lives, in their position . . . I'd murder, steal, cheat. Of course, I would. It's all because I wasn't in their position. I was in mine.

Valentine watches him attentively, and slowly comes two steps closer.

VALENTINE

Is there someone you love?

JUDGE

No.

VALENTINE

Has there been?

After a while, the Judge, seeing Valentine's wide-open, serious eyes gazing at him, speaks.

JUDGE

I had a nice dream last night. I dreamt of you. You were forty or fifty and happy.

VALENTINE
Do your dreams come true?

JUDGE
I haven't had a nice dream for years.

INT. AUGUST'S FLAT. NIGHT

August, in shirt and braces, is pacing up and down his flat. He is acting like a prisoner – two steps forward, three steps back. He sits down at his desk. He lights a cigarette and, even before having taken a puff, immediately stubs it out. He gets up and starts walking again but immediately stops. He picks up the telephone and calls, knowing the number by heart. Just as when he was in the courts, and again no one picks up the phone. August holds the receiver to his ear for a very long time. Finally, he throws it back on the hook and, grabbing his jacket in flight, runs out of the flat.

INT. STAIRWELL BY AUGUST'S FLAT. NIGHT

August, several steps at a time, dashes down the stairs. He runs out.

EXT. IN FRONT OF AUGUST'S FLAT. NIGHT

August gets in his car, closes the door with force. He has caught his jacket, so opens the door again, tugs at the jacket and slams the door. He turns on the engine, moves off. Paying no attention to traffic regulations, he drives across the stretch of grass dividing the road.

EXT. CITY STREETS. NIGHT

August leaves the city centre, arrives in the villa neighbourhood. He passes the Judge's house. The camera stops briefly at the house we know so well. We see the silhouette of a man (the Judge) standing in the window. We cannot make his face out easily. It is the only window with a light on among the houses near by. August drives a little further and brakes in front of a multi-storeyed building. He does not make any noise now. He shuts the door carefully and quietly climbs the stairs.

INT. STAIRWELL TO KARIN'S FLAT. NIGHT

August climbs to the second floor on tiptoe. He nears a door which he

clearly knows and puts his ear to it. For a moment, he hesitates whether to knock, decides not to. He listens carefully again; obviously hears what he was afraid of because he turns pale. After a moment's thought, he goes up to the stairwell window, opens it and climbs out.

INT./EXT. BUILDING FAÇADE AND KARIN'S FLAT. NIGHT

Holding on to the protruding parapet, August makes his way, step by step, along the ledge of the building. Slowly, he nears the illuminated window. He closes his eyes, then opens them resolutely and, as if he were about to jump to the pavement from a great height, leans out to look through the window. A spasm wrecks his face, but he does not close his eyes or turn away. On a wide, clearly visible bed, Karin is lying with a man. There can be no doubt as to what they are doing. August, his eyes wide open, presses his face to the wall.

INT./EXT. VALENTINE'S FLAT. DAY

Valentine, still in bed, is talking over the telephone.

VALENTINE

I've bought a ticket for the ferry . . .

*She reaches for her handbag which is lying by the bed. She pulls the
ticket out, a newspaper falls to the floor. Valentine checks the details on
the ticket.*

Wednesday week. I'll be in England at two-thirty in the
afternoon.

MICHEL
(*off*)

Why the ferry?

VALENTINE

I'll pop into Mum's for a day. It's only a couple of hours from
there to Calais.

MICHEL
(*off*)

I'll be at the harbour at three, latest three-thirty. I'm glad
you're coming.

VALENTINE

Tell me, Michel . . . Do you love me?

MICHEL
(*off*)

I think so.

VALENTINE

Do you love me or do you think so?

MICHEL
(*off*)

Same thing.

Pause.

VALENTINE

No.

MICHEL
(*off*)

Valentine . . . I'm looking forward to seeing you.

See you, then.

Valentine replaces the receiver, pushes the sheet aside and lies there in only her nightdress for a while. It is cold and a shudder runs down her spine. She gets up, goes to the window. She watches the street for a while. It is early in the morning. She sees a jeep come to a stop several doors down on the other side of the street. Even though it is daylight, the jeep has its headlights on. Nobody gets out, the silhouette of a man (August) rages behind the steering wheel. Valentine turns away from the window and goes to the kitchen. She tips some coffee into the filter, pours some water in and turns on the machine.

EXT. IN FRONT OF AUGUST'S FLAT. DAY

The door of the jeep with headlights on opens. August gets out, does not turn the lights off. Slowly, he enters his building.

INT. STAIRWELL TO AUGUST'S FLAT. DAY

August heavily climbs the stairs.

INT. AUGUST'S FLAT. DAY

The dog leaps up when August opens the door. Obviously wanting to go for a walk, it holds the leash between its teeth. August does not pay it any attention and, without undressing, collapses on the bed. The dog stands with its front paws on the bed. It wants to lick August; it wags its tail. August thumps the dog hard in the snout. The dog jumps away, squealing. August buries his head in the pillow and freezes.

INT. VALENTINE'S FLAT. DAY

Valentine, after her bath, her hair wet, pours some coffee from the steaming machine. She wraps her hands around the hot mug and, sipping, walks up to the window. She sees the jeep standing in the same place with its headlights still on. There is nobody inside.

VALENTINE
(*murmurs*)

The battery . . .

She adjusts a falling lock of hair and, all the while watching the jeep with its headlights on, stays in this position. She remains like this for a while.

INT./EXT. JUDGE'S HOUSE. DAY

The Judge is standing by the broken window. He is gazing ahead of himself. What he notices draws his attention. A young man is leaving the distant multi-storeyed building. Even from this distance, it is possible to see that he is in a good mood. He searches for puddles in the road and jumps into them purposely, splashing the water. He runs quickly for a while, disappears down the road. The Judge has been watching him carefully. Now he goes to the telephone and dials. Karin answers.

> KARIN
> (*off*)

Good morning. Detailed weather report.

> JUDGE

I've been trying to get through to you for several days.

> KARIN
> (*off*)

I was ill. I'm sorry.

> JUDGE

Could you tell me, please, what the weather's going to be like over the English Channel next week.

> KARIN
> (*off*)

Beautiful. Sunny, a slight breeze, cold in the morning . . .

She starts laughing for no reason.

> JUDGE

Why are you laughing?

> KARIN
> (*off*)

I'm going that way. Even further.

> JUDGE

Work?

KARIN
(*off*)

Pure pleasure. On a yacht.

JUDGE

That's a beautiful sail . . .

KARIN
(*off*)

Yes, beautiful.

JUDGE

Are you going to be closing the office?

KARIN
(*off*)

I'll have to.

JUDGE

Pity. It's been a good idea. Goodbye.

KARIN
(*off*)

Goodbye.

The Judge replaces the receiver. He hides the bottle of pear brandy in its place, screens it with books. He goes through to the bedroom, leans over the cot. Rita is licking her pups with her wide tongue. She looks at the Judge, proud of her young ones. The Judge smiles.

JUDGE

What're we going to do with your little ones, Rita?

The bitch gazes at him as if she understood the gravity of the question.

INT./EXT. CITY STREET. NIGHT

August is sitting in his car, parked in a side street. He is in his shirt, his jacket undone. He glances at his watch, holding it under the light of a street café. He nods, it is time. He gets out. He moves in the direction of a clearly visible, illuminated café. He approaches the café window, finds what he was looking for.

INT./EXT. CAFÉ. NIGHT

Inside, near the window, Karin is sitting with her new Boyfriend. The man has an intelligent, pleasant, lively face. He is holding Karin's hand. Karin is laughing, so is he. August watches this, his head pressed against the window. This goes on for some time. The man takes some photographs from his wallet and shows them to Karin. The photographs depict a beautiful, large yacht in different places: southern seas in a storm; the yacht sailing and moored by the shore; scenes of diving. Some of them must be funny because they keep bursting out laughing. August puts his hand on the window and taps. Immersed in conversation, they obviously do not see him. August smiles unpleasantly and pulls out the fountain pen which – as we remember – he received as a present from Karin. He uses it to tap on the window – it is more effective. The man raises his eyes and looks at him, not understanding. August continues tapping. The man touches Karin's hand and points to the window. Karin freezes. August stops tapping. Karin watches his face, aghast. She gets up without saying anything and pushes her way to the exit. It is quite a long way. She steps outside.

EXT. IN FRONT OF THE CAFÉ. NIGHT

Karin looks around, August has disappeared. She runs up to the window, he is not there either.

> KARIN
> (*shouts*)

August!

No one answers.

> (*shouts desperatelty*)

August! Auguuuuuuust!

August, hiding behind a post near by, does not move. His teeth are chattering.

INT. THEATRE WINGS. DAY

The mayhem of a fashion show rehearsal in the theatre wings. The theatre is old fashioned with ornate balconies, red plush seating and a tiered amphitheatre-like auditorium. Construction of the catwalk running from the stage into the audience is just finishing. On the stage: railings of coat hangers, evening gowns, hats spread out everywhere possible. Models, helpers, technicians. At a small table, a Woman is sorting out administrative matters. Valentine walks up to her with a small card in her hand.

VALENTINE

I've got a favour to ask. Could you please send an invitation to this address?

The Woman examines the card. She makes sure.

WOMAN

Just one person?

Valentine nods, just one.

INT. CAFÉ. NIGHT

The coloured barrels of the one-armed bandit revolve. They stop at three different pictures. Valentine breathes a sigh of relief. As usual, she exchanges a thumbs-up with the Barman – 'Everything's going to be okay!'

INT./EXT. JUDGE'S GARAGE. DAY

Darkness. The garage doors slowly rise. An old, well-kept Mercedes drives out. It stops; the dark smoke of a long-disused car flows from the exhaust. The Judge, in suit and bow-tie, gets out and lowers the garage door.

EXT. CITY STREETS. DAY

Slowly and carefully, the old Mercedes makes its way through the city streets. It passes – in the opposite direction to August's jeep – by the building under renovation with its photograph of Valentine chewing gum, which is now a little weatherbeaten. The Judge turns to take a look at the photograph, the building with the ad disappears in the rear window. The Mercedes drives up to the theatre and parks, carefully leaving ample room on both sides.

INT. THEATRE. DAY

The fashion show is in progress. There are a lot of people in the

audience. *Valentine, together with her colleagues, steps out on to the catwalk. As at the beginning of the film, they move gracefully, energetically. To the rhythm of the music, they walk forward together a dozen or so steps. Valentine searches for someone in the audience. She does not lose the rhythm and performs everything according to plan, but when they disperse at the end of the catwalk, she again tries to catch sight of someone in the audience. She does not find that person. On her way back, she looks at the people on the other side of the auditorium. The person she would like to see is not there either. When they step into the wings and a new group of models walks out, Valentine peers at the audience through a gap in the wings. She goes up to the Woman from administration.*

VALENTINE

Did you send out that invitation I asked you to yesterday?

WOMAN

Of course, Valentine.

Valentine washes the lipstick off her mouth, puts on her own coat and leaves the dressing-room with several of her colleagues. They cross the stage where the spotlights have already been extinguished, descend the steps to the auditorium divided by the catwalk. They make their way to the exit, discussing the show. Valentine, lagging behind a little, is not taking part in the conversation. All the doors of the auditorium are open – we see the corridors and open windows. Valentine suddenly stops. She catches sight of the Judge sitting alone at the back of the auditorium. Valentine's colleagues have not noticed that she has stopped, and leave. Valentine remains in the hall with the Judge. The Judge stands in greeting. Valentine walks over to him across the long hall.

VALENTINE

You came . . . Did you know that the invitation was from me?

JUDGE

I wanted it to be.

Valentine nods, amused.

You were looking for me.

VALENTINE

Right through the show. I'm leaving tomorrow. It's time to say goodbye . . .

The Judge holds out his hand.

JUDGE

Goodbye.

Valentine holds out hers and, for a while, holds the Judge's hand.

VALENTINE

I'd like you to describe your dream to me in detail. The one
about me . . .

JUDGE

I told you. You were fifty and happy.

*Valentine, hoisting herself up a little with her hands, sits on the
podium. The Judge sits on one of the seats near Valentine, a little lower
down.*

VALENTINE

In that dream . . . was there anybody else?

JUDGE

There was.

VALENTINE

Who?

JUDGE

You woke up and smiled at somebody lying beside you. I
don't know who.

VALENTINE

Is that going to happen? In twenty or twenty-five years' time?

JUDGE

Yes.

Valentine moves away from the Judge.

VALENTINE
(*quietly*)

What else do you know?

The Judge does not answer.

(*quietly*)
Who are you?

The Judge smiles faintly.

JUDGE
A retired judge.

VALENTINE
I've got a feeling that something important is happening around me. And I'm scared.

The Judge holds his hand out to Valentine. She does not understand what he wants, then gives him her hand. The Judge holds her palm in his hands for a while.

JUDGE
Better.

Valentine smiles, better.

I often used to come to this theatre.

VALENTINE
Where did you usually sit?

The Judge points up to the balcony.

JUDGE
The same place as today. That's why you didn't see me. Once, during the interval, my books fell all over the place. They were held together by an elastic band. One of them, a thick one, fell down below. Somewhere here . . .

The Judge takes a few steps forwards and stands at the orchestra pit. He looks up and gauges where his book would have fallen years ago. He finds it.

It was just before my exam. The book had fallen open on a certain page. I read a few sentences. They proved useful. I was able to answer a difficult question in the exam.

Valentine watches the lively Judge show her where his book had fallen into the orchestra pit and relive the situation when he picked it up and read it. She goes up to the Judge, gracefully climbing over the seats.

VALENTINE
It's good you've gone out, isn't it?

JUDGE
I even recharged the battery. It had gone flat . . .

At that moment, we hear the door slam. A draught starts up, the sky through the open corridor windows has become overcast, a sudden, spring downpour arises.

VALENTINE
There's a storm.

She rushes towards the corridor and closes the open windows, one by one. Heavy rain lashes against the windows.

EXT. CITY STREETS. DAY

August stands in the street under a large, dark umbrella. He is waiting. The rain is cutting but August stands motionless, does not run to hide in gateways or under bus shelters as do all the other passers-by. His face is determined. Karin emerges from the subway on the other side of the street. She is quite far from August but notices him immediately in the deserted street. She ignores the rain. She walks, not very fast, towards him. August, too, takes a few steps in her direction. Karin stops two steps in front of him. Very slowly, August takes these two steps. They look each other in the eye for some time without a word. August's lips are trembling a little, perhaps from the cold. Raindrops trickle down his face. Karin's hair is drenched. Only able to bear August's gaze for a certain length of time, she lowers her eyes. August then bows his head and rests it on her shoulder. Karin stares ahead of her, neither hugs him to her nor pushes him away. She is unable to do anything. She speaks helplessly, rather quietly.

KARIN
I love him . . .

Initially it seems that August has not heard. But he has because, without moving his head from Karin's shoulder, he speaks quietly, almost to himself.

AUGUST
Oh, God . . .

They stay in this position for another dozen or so seconds and then Karin gently frees herself and slowly walks away. The rain is still pouring down. Karin walks away at a steady pace without looking back. August remains with his head bowed, under his umbrella. He takes the fountain pen from his pocket and throws it into a nearby bin. We stay with the bin for a while. We hear steps approach and see a hand fish the pen out from the bin.

INT. THEATRE. DAY/DUSK

The Judge presses a button and coffee pours into two plastic cups from the machine in the theatre foyer. The Judge picks them up and, passing through the corridor where the sudden rain is still lashing against the windows, enters the auditorium. Valentine is no longer where she was sitting before.

> JUDGE
> (*quietly*)
> Valentine . . . Valentine!

Valentine answers from the balcony which the Judge had pointed to before.

> VALENTINE
> I'm here . . .

The Judge looks up. Valentine leans over the balcony.

> JUDGE
> Watch out . . . you're very high up.

Valentine pulls the newspaper out of her pocket, holds it between two fingers and lets it go. The paper, circling in the air, floats to the floor. It lands in the orchestra pit.

> VALENTINE
> Was that it? Is that where it landed?

> JUDGE
> Yes.

He makes his way towards the orchestra pit, taking care not to spill the coffee. He opens the small gate. As he is crossing the conductor's podium, he is stopped by Valentine's voice.

VALENTINE

Was it a fashion show?

JUDGE

No. They were playing Molière. *Le Misanthrope.*

The Judge leaves the plastic cups on the conductor's music stand and walks further down. He squats, folds the newspaper. A woman's hands gather the cups and we see Valentine descend the steps and sit on an old seat by the Judge as he picks up the paper. When the Judge, surprised by her presence, turns towards her, Valentine passes him a cup.

VALENTINE

Thank you.

She smells her coffee. The Judge sits on the podium.

JUDGE

Pretty mediocre.

In the shadows, the theatre's machinery rumbles, red lights shine. Valentine takes a couple of sips of her coffee, grimaces, it is not very good.

VALENTINE

I was wondering. Why did you tell me that story about the sailor . . .

JUDGE

Do you know why?

Valentine takes a last sip and squashes the cup in her hand. The typical crack of plastic. She examines the cracked cup.

VALENTINE

Yes. Because you didn't want to tell me something more important.

Valentine lifts her eyes from the squashed, crackling cup up to the Judge only at the last moment. The Judge is looking straight at her.

About a woman you loved.

The Judge nods.

She betrayed you.

Again the Judge slowly nods.

> She betrayed you . . . and you couldn't understand why.

The Judge nods.

> You kept on loving her for a long time.

The Judge now looks at her, motionless, neither affirming nor denying.

JUDGE
How do you know so much?

Valentine smiles.

VALENTINE
It wasn't hard to guess.

She leans over and is now near the Judge.

> What was she like?

JUDGE
She was blonde. Delicate, fair, with a long neck. She wore
light-coloured dresses . . . Had light-coloured furniture. A
mirror in a white frame hung in the hallway. In that mirror one
night I saw her white legs spread, with a man between them.

VALENTINE
Why? Do you know?

JUDGE
She wanted more than I could offer. She thought she loved
me, but she didn't want peace and quiet . . . she liked to wake
up in foreign places. I wanted only the security of tomorrow.
Hugo Holbling . . . that was his name . . . gave her what she
wanted. They left. I followed them. I crossed France, the
Channel, saw Scotland, even further . . . I humiliated myself
and was humiliated right up until the moment she died in an
accident. Then I never got involved with another woman.
Yes, I stopped believing. Or maybe I simply didn't meet . . .
maybe I didn't meet you?

VALENTINE
Why didn't you meet me?

282

JUDGE

Because you didn't exist then.

EXT. SUBURBS OF GENEVA. DUSK

It has stopped raining, only drops fall from branches. With the red leash August carefully ties his black, shaggy dog to a post some yards away from the kerb of a suburban street. The dog, surprised, observes this new situation. August, without looking back and with determination, walks away to his car. Hearing the frightened dog bark and squeal, he blocks his ears. He gets into his jeep and drives off as fast as he can. He drives a couple of hundred yards and abruptly brakes. He puts the car into reverse and backs back. He reverses on to the pavement near the post with the tied dog. He gets out, unties the dog which immediately forgives him. He opens the back door of the jeep and the dog, now calm, jumps into its usual place. August gets into the car and moves off.

INT. THEATRE. DUSK

The Judge and Valentine are still sitting in the same position we left them in a moment ago. Valentine tears the Judge away from his thoughts.

VALENTINE

That's not the end . . .

JUDGE

No. A year ago I got a difficult case. On it was written the name of the defendant: Hugo Holbling.

VALENTINE

The same man?

JUDGE

Yes. He'd come back here . . .

We hear a man's heavy footsteps approach. The Judge grows silent. The theatre Watchman appears from the depths of the stage. He is rattling dozens of keys on a keyring. He notices someone sitting in the wings and stops. He switches on the working light and comes closer.

WATCHMAN

I'm locking up.

The Judge and Valentine get up.

You haven't seen a woman with a bucket, have you?

VALENTINE

No.

WATCHMAN

The storm has flooded the dressing-rooms. Tell her I'm upstairs if you see her.

Valentine nods. The Watchman, rattling his keys, disappears into the wings. The Judge makes as if to go. After a few steps, he realizes that Valentine has not moved. He turns to her questioningly.

VALENTINE

You should have given that case up.

JUDGE

I didn't want to.

VALENTINE

What did you do?

JUDGE

I wanted to kill him at one time and probably would have if it could have changed anything. Now he was waiting for my verdict. He was in charge of the construction of a hall which collapsed. Several people were killed. I pronounced him guilty. He didn't manage to appeal. The day after he was sentenced, he died of a heart attack . . .

VALENTINE

In jail?

JUDGE

No. It was a suspended sentence.

VALENTINE

Did he know it was you?

JUDGE

He didn't.

Valentine comes closer. She looks at the Judge tensely.

When I read his name in the case file, I realized that I'd been waiting for a moment like this. The sentence was according to law . . .

The Judge chuckles briefly, unpleasantly.

But I had a nice feeling of revenge during the trial. Then I requested early retirement . . .

Valentine nods, she has understood. Again we hear the Watchman's approaching footsteps and the rattle of keys. He appears from the wings.

WATCHMAN
Hasn't she been here?

JUDGE
No.

The Watchman nods, displeased.

WATCHMAN
I'm always having to traipse around after her.

He walks away into the depths of the auditorium, shouting.

Milana! Milaaana!!

The Judge smiles, so does Valentine. The Watchman leaves the hall, unhurried. They both watch his amusing silhouette disappear into the darkness.

VALENTINE
You've been without love all your life.

JUDGE
Yes.

EXT. IN FRONT OF THE THEATRE. NIGHT

The Judge opens the boot of his Mercedes, which is parked in front of the theatre. He takes out a plastic bag, hands it to Valentine. She touches the bag, feels a bottle inside.

JUDGE
You liked my pear brandy.

VALENTINE

Thank you. There's just one more thing I'd like to ask you.

JUDGE

Yes?

VALENTINE

I'll probably be away for two or three weeks. Then I'll give you a call. I'd like you to give me one of your puppies.

JUDGE

Will the fashion show be on TV?

VALENTINE

I think so.

The Judge smiles an unexpectedly young smile.

JUDGE

I'd better buy myself a TV.

VALENTINE

I've got one which I don't need. I'll ask my brother to bring it over tomorrow.

The Judge smiles like he did before.

JUDGE

I'd like to meet him. I'll see you soon.

VALENTINE

See you.

The Judge shuts the boot, gets into the car. He lowers the window.

JUDGE

Do you have your ticket with you?

Valentine, surprised, rummages in her bag. She pulls out the ferry ticket. The Judge stretches out his hand through the window. Valentine hands him the ticket. The Judge examines it for a moment in the poor light of the car. He gives the ticket back to Valentine, winds his window up and puts his palm up against it. Valentine brings her palm up to the same place. The Judge moves off. He passes a jeep going the other way. Valentine crosses the square to where her car is parked. She opens the door, her eyes follow the Judge who is driving away with dignity. The Judge's car passes a green container for recycled bottles. An old, well-dressed, hunched woman is approaching the container with a bottle in her hand. She gets up on tiptoes. The bottle slips in only halfway, the woman cannot push it right through the rubber collar. Valentine, seeing her attempts, runs a few yards and, with one move, pushes the bottle into the container. We hear the tinkle of broken glass.

EXT. FERRY HARBOUR. DAY

A long queue of passengers climb the metal stairs to the ferry. Valentine, with a rucksack and a small suitcase, disappears into the dark interior. She is followed by a middle-aged couple, two laughing, chattering girls and then August. He has taken his black dog, which is obviously scared of the steep stairs, into his arms.

INT. FERRY. DAY

The reception desk is located directly in front of the entrance to the ferry. Valentine, glancing at her ticket, climbs the stairs to the upper deck. The married couple come down, stopping briefly at reception. The chattering girls climb the stairs after Valentine. August stands the dog on the floor and goes up to reception. He shows his ticket. The Receptionist points out the direction.

> RECEPTIONIST
> That's on this deck. This corridor.

August looks down the corridor. He moves off. At that same moment, Valentine appears at the top of the stairs. She comes down, goes to reception.

> VALENTINE
> I can't find my way . . . where is this? F38?

> RECEPTIONIST
> The deck above.

August stops halfway down the corridor. He looks around, his eyes half-conscious. Valentine smiles at the Receptionist. Meanwhile, other passengers mill around.

VALENTINE

Thank you.

August takes a step towards reception. At that moment, Valentine turns her back and climbs the same stairs for a second time. August has obviously realized that he had taken the right direction because he turns round again and moves away down the corridor. They were perhaps three or five steps away from each other. Now they have gone in different directions.

EXT. FERRY HARBOUR. DAY

The huge ferry majestically pulls away from the harbour.

EXT. CITY STREET. DAY

The renovation of the building is obviously complete because workers are lowering the enormous canvas – with the photograph of Valentine chewing gum – which covered the multi-storeyed scaffolding. The photograph frowns, folds and slowly slides down to the street. The workers, hampered by the rising wind, start to fold up the canvas. Clouds of dust appear above the canvas. Heavy drops of rain begin to fall. We hear the first rolls of thunder, see flashes of lightning. The rain grows stronger, it grows dark. Downpour. Streams of rain splatter over the outspread canvas. Thunder. Darkness.

INT./EXT. FERRY/SEA. SPECIAL EFFECTS. ARCHIVE MATERIAL. NIGHT

The light goes out and the desperate shouting of masses of people is intensified. We hear people running in all directions. The crack of metal breaking; another explosion; a column of fire; the faces of terrified people fly across the screen; bodies fall. Amid explosions, the powerful, enormous, dark hulk sinks into the stormy water.

INT. JUDGE'S HOUSE. DAY

Early morning. The Judge, having just woken up, observes a pup which has, with difficulty – probably for the first time – climbed the cot partition. With outspread paws, it holds on to the board. Losing its balance, it sways this way and that, and finally makes a decision: it jumps down clumsily on to the carpet. The Judge gets up and fastens a collar with a metal name tag – which he had clearly prepared earlier – around its neck. He puts the pup back in the cot. He goes out into the hallway and finds a newspaper which the postman has dropped in. He opens the door, breathes in the morning air for a moment, the weather is good. Puddles glisten after yesterday's downpour. He glances at the paper and freezes. There is a large headline on the front page and a blurred, technically poor photograph. The Judge, in disbelief, slowly lifts the paper closer to his eyes.

EXT. LAKESIDE. DAY

A newspaper carried by a Boy in the open air by a lake. In the background – by the shore – there are several sleeping-bags and primitive tents with people sleeping inside. The Boy with the paper shakes the owner of one of the sleeping-bags. He wakes him. A sixteen-year-old boy with a pleasant face, Marc, reluctantly opens his eyes. The Boy shoves the paper under his nose.

BOY

Have you seen this?

Marc, freshly awake, is not entirely conscious. He does not know what they want from him.

MARC

What?

The Boy opens the first page of the paper. The headline is: 'TRAGEDY ON THE ENGLISH CHANNEL'.

BOY

Your sister survived.

Marc comes to.

MARC

What?

BOY

They're writing about your sister. She survived the disaster. Only a few people did. The rest drowned . . .

Marc bends over the paper.

INT. JUDGE'S HOUSE. NIGHT

TV screen. Photographs (archive material, video) of the ferry wreck sticking out of the sea, absurd objects, which usually survive a disastrous shipwreck, tossed about by the waves. We see ships and rescue launches circling near by.

COMMENTARY
(off)

. . . very bad weather conditions and storms on the English Channel made rescue operations difficult. A private sailing yacht sank at the same time. The cause of the ferry disaster is not, as yet, known. According to the passenger list there were 1,435 passengers on board. A Norwegian ship, responding to the SOS, retrieved seven people and these have, in all certainty, survived.

The TV camera shows the people descending to the shore, wrapped in blankets. It stops at each of the faces, accompanied by a commentary.

The widow of the eminent French composer who died last year, Julie Vignon.

Julie's face held in frame for a moment.

Stephen Killian, British citizen, barman on the ferry. A Polish businessman, Karol Karol.

Karol's face.

French citizen Dominique Vidal.

Dominique's face.

Frenchman Olivier Benoit.

Olivier's face.

Among the survivors are also two Swiss citizens. August Bruner, lawyer.

August's face.

And young model, a student at the University of Geneva, Valentine Dussaut.

Valentine's face. She adjusts a lock of hair. The Judge, sitting in front of his TV, watches her. Valentine moves off. She joins the small group of survivors surrounded by coast-guards, journalists and officials. She stands beside August.

FADE OUT.

Against a black background: END CREDITS.

The Films of Krzysztof Kieślowski

ART 085

Three Colours Blue

Juliette Binoche is stunning in this compelling psychological drama about a composer's widow exploring her newfound freedom.
'Classic Kieślowski... beautiful'
Independent on Sunday

ART 024A

Dekalog 1-5

A landmark in cinema history, these short films, loosely based on the Ten Commandments, received glowing praise and numerous awards.
'Each film is a miniature jewel'
Sunday Times

ART 100

Three Colours White

The second in Kieślowski's award-winning trilogy is a very funny and ironic black comedy set in Paris and Warsaw.
'Compulsively watchable... outstanding' Observer

ART 024A

Dekalog 6-10

The final five films in the series explore the universal themes of love, marriage, guilt, faith and compassion.
'A work of classic stature' The Times

ART 105

Three Colours Red

The third and most powerful in Kieślowski's trilogy is an outstanding film on the theme of brotherhood, starring Irène Jacob and Jean-Louis Trintignant.
'Towering achievement... astonishing' Time Out
OUT MARCH 1995

'Europe's premier director' The Guardian

Artificial Eye Collection